Cambrid

Elements in ...
edited by
James R. Lewis
Wuhan University
Margo Kitts
Hawai'i Pacific University

VIOLATED AND TRANSCENDED BODIES

Gender, Martyrdom, and Asceticism in Early Christianity

Gail P. Streete

Rhodes College

CAMBRIDGE
UNIVERSITY PRESS

CAMBRIDGE
UNIVERSITY PRESS

University Printing House, Cambridge CB2 8BS, United Kingdom

One Liberty Plaza, 20th Floor, New York, NY 10006, USA

477 Williamstown Road, Port Melbourne, VIC 3207, Australia

314–321, 3rd Floor, Plot 3, Splendor Forum, Jasola District Centre,
New Delhi – 110025, India

79 Anson Road, #06–04/06, Singapore 079906

Cambridge University Press is part of the University of Cambridge.

It furthers the University's mission by disseminating knowledge in the pursuit of
education, learning, and research at the highest international levels of excellence.

www.cambridge.org
Information on this title: www.cambridge.org/9781009054157
DOI: 10.1017/9781009053372

First published 2021

A catalogue record for this publication is available from the British Library.

ISBN 978-1-009-05415-7 Paperback
ISSN 2397-9496 (online)
ISSN 2514-3786 (print)

Violated and Transcended Bodies

Gender, Martyrdom, and Asceticism in Early Christianity

Elements in Religion and Violence

DOI: 10.1017/9781009053372
First published online: May 2021

Gail P. Streete
Rhodes College

Author for correspondence: Gail P. Streete, gstreete1@comcast.net

ABSTRACT: Given its eschatological orientation and its marginal position in the Roman Empire, emergent Christianity found embodiment, as an aspect of being in the world, problematic. Those identified and identifying as Christians developed two broad responses to that world as they embraced the idea of being in, yet not of, it. The first response, martyrdom, was witness to the strength their faith gave to fragile bodies, particularly those of women, and the ability by suffering to overcome bodily limitation and attain the resurrection life. The second, asceticism, complemented and later continued martyrdom as a means of bodily transcendence and participation in the spiritual world.

KEYWORDS: asceticism, concepts of body, early Christianity, gender, martyrdom

ISBNs: 9781009054157 (PB), 9781009053372 (OC)
ISSNs: 2397-9496 (online), 2514-3786 (print)

Contents

1 About Bodies, Gender, and Identity

This Element is about embodiment (Streete, 2009: 12). Specifically, it is about the way in which bodies are used as symbolic arenas for the performance of identity and vehicles for the inscription of that identity: in this case, a Christian one (Streete, 2018: 40).[1] Given its orientation toward the end of the present age, and its marginal position in the Roman Empire, emergent Christianity found embodiment a problematic aspect of being in the world. Christians developed two broad responses to that world as they embraced the idea of being in, yet not of, it. The first response, martyrdom, was a testimony to the strength their faith leant to fragile bodies, particularly those of women, perceived as the "weaker sex" (1 Pet 3:7), and the ability to overcome bodily limitation to attain the resurrection life, one that was conceived of as being in a bodily, if not fleshly, form. As will be shown in Section 3.2, Candida Moss (2019) demonstrates how hazy this idea of "bodily" form was in early Christianity.

The second response, asceticism, complemented and later continued martyrdom as a means of bodily transcendence, with participation in the spiritual world while still in the physical flesh, which was perceived as either a burden or an envelope. As Sebastian Brock and Susan Ashbrook Harvey (1987: 14) remark,

> Martyrdom and asceticism are two forms of the same event: humanity's encounter with the divine, specifically through the imitation of Christ, God incarnate. In times of peace it is the saint's *Life* that is shown to mirror the work of Christ, usually with asceticism providing the manner of imitation. In times of persecution, it is the saint's death, or rather the manner of the saint's death, that proves significant: martyrs' passions pivot on that event and what led up to it.

---

[1] While early Christianity was not monolithic, so that one might more properly speak of "Christianities," discourses about martyrdom and ascetic behavior were shared by several varieties of Christianity, even those that might oppose them as deviating from "true" Christianity.

As Mary Douglas (1996: 65) famously observed, bodily representation is inseparable from the society in which those bodies are located: "The social body constrains the way the physical body is perceived. The physical experience of the body, always modified by the social categories through which it is known, sustains a particular view of society." The microcosmic body reflects the macrocosmic society (its universe), and vice versa. Whatever form of Christianity they practiced, early Christians thought a good deal about bodies, their thinking developing from the intersection of cultures in which Christianity as a distinct religion emerged. From Judaism, Christianity developed the idea of the person as a living being, an animate entity made in God's image, one that God had endowed with breath (Gen 2:7), and, later, one that would be raised by God with the righteous in some recognizable, perhaps bodily form (4 Macc 18:17–19). In Hellenism, particularly in Greek philosophy and medicine, Christian writers and theologians found the concept of the "soul" (*psychē*), usually identified with mind or intelligence, and the mind's often problematic relationship to the body, in which the body, characterized as *sarx*, or flesh, and its passions could prove an impediment to the soul and its reasoning powers. The Roman contribution to Christian thinking about bodies seems to have been one of display or spectacle: captive bodies marched in the triumphs of victorious Roman generals, or the disposable bodies on show in the arena in the *agon* (struggle or contest), to be dispatched by gladiators or beasts: "For the Romans . . . killing was not clandestine, nor was it to be ignored: the killers, the killing, the dying and the dead all were to be seen" (Kyle, 1998: 2). Yet from the Romans also, via Greco-Roman Stoicism, came the performance known as the heroic or noble death, the release of the embattled soul from the body by one's own hand at the appropriate moment. Marcus Aurelius (*Meditations* 11.3) claimed that noble suicide had to be "without theatrics," exhibiting an aristocratic Roman distaste for Christian martyrdoms (Droge and Tabor, 1992: 162). What the average person may have thought or felt about their bodies is unclear, since most of our evidence comes from texts written by the literate, but one thing is certain: bodies and their breakability and expendability were visibly present on a daily basis in the social and political realms of slavery, warfare, childbirth, gladiatorial combat, executions, and routine torture of slaves and criminals.

For the early Christians, as for their contemporaries, "Bodies mattered as much … as they do now – and particular bodies mattered more and embodied more power and authority than others" (Vander Stichele and Penner, 2009: 40–1). Bodies, moreover, had status as well as gender. For example, slaves were routinely referred to as "the bodies, *ta sōmata*" in Greek (Glancy, 2002: 10). Even when the Roman Empire became Christian, the bodies of female slaves and those of the underclasses (the *humiliores*) were not expected to be held in the same honor as those of the freeborn and upper classes (*honestiores*): as Theodosian Codex 9.7.1 (326 CE) indicates, the virtue of chastity was neither expected nor possible for these lower-class women because of their "worthless life" (Brown, 1988: 24).[2] The ancients also understood the concept of "performing gender" long before postmodernism used the phrase and did not employ a strict gender binary, using a sliding scale or spectrum of masculinity and femininity, but this is not to say that women's and men's bodies remained physically undifferentiated, at least in the literature. As Vander Stichele and Penner (2009: 67) note, "Gender [in the ancient world] was not so much a given, but rather something that had to be acquired and proven," by demonstration and observation. Gender, in other words, was performed. Bodies perceived as passive, ones that could be dominated and penetrated, whether male or female, were defined as "feminine," while those that were active and dominant were defined as "masculine" (Vander Stichele and Penner, 2009: 61). Torture was a violation of the body that made even male bodies technically female but could also make female bodies male through their steadfast endurance of pain (B. Shaw, 1996: 293). In the *Martydom of Perpetua and Felicitas*, for example, Felicitas' birth pains are portrayed as more painful than what she will endure in the arena (*Martyrdom*, 15.6), childbirth being an ancient site of pain and the need for endurance for women, as envisioned by men. Euripides' Medea declares, "I would very much rather stand three times in the front of battle than bear one child" (*Medea*, 250–1).

---

[2] For a more developed discussion of the intersection of gender and class in martyrdom and asceticism, see Section 4.1, "Bodies and Status."

The body itself was classically understood as having two and possibly three components or realms: *sarx*, the flesh, which humans shared with animals; *psychē*, mind or soul; and *pneuma*, spirit or breath, an element that humans sometimes shared with the divine life, along with the *psychē*'s ability to reason. The fleshly part of the person was linked to the passions; the mind, if properly developed, was the seat of rationality and could control the body and its passions, as in Plato's Allegory of the Charioteer (*Phaedrus*, 246 c–254 c); while the spirit was the immortal part of the person, sometimes identified as soul, but in Jewish and Christian teaching, as the divine breath that God shared with human beings (Gen 1:26–27). Like their Greek and Roman contemporaries, the early Christians often saw the domain of flesh as inimical to that of the spirit, which was allied with God (Miles, 2013: 142). In its most extreme expression, found in some forms of Gnosticism, with its emphasis on the division between material and spiritual, this conflict was outright warfare: the true human, like the Divine, inhabited the spiritual realm, even while physically in the flesh, and any regard for the realm of the flesh – the material world – was a form of delusion. Some Gnostic Christians[3] even inveighed against martyrdom, the use of the body as a form of testimony, as a cruel deception about the means of redemption. In the Coptic *Apocalypse of Peter* (6. 79. 22–31), for example, Christians are deceived into thinking that they imitate Christ in their deaths – an essential feature of martyrdom – when in fact the "living Savior" is "glad and laughing" (Streete, 2018: 42). Nonetheless, the orthodox Christian teachers and theologians[4] who later dominated Christianity could not depict the flesh or the body, the entity that held together flesh and spirit, as wholly evil and still subscribe to the canonical view that God had created a good material universe that included human beings along with their mortal bodies. Because of their Greek philosophical studies, however, they struggled

---

[3] "Gnostic" in this context refers to those who believe that we are saved by the secret knowledge the "Savior" (Jesus) came to impart: that the true human in the image of God is spirit.

[4] "Orthodox" refers primarily to the Christian beliefs as developed in the third to eighth centuries, based on creeds, an accepted canon, and several Ecumenical (worldwide Christian) councils.

with this concept. Given the evidence of the gospels and the letters of Paul, these theologians had to understand the body of Christ as sacrificed, dead, and buried, which rose in bodily form, and as the body celebrated as redemptive in the ritual of the Eucharist. In the end, by attaching desire to the unruly flesh (*sarx*), they managed to exempt Jesus Christ, though incarnate, from human desire, and also to problematize human sexuality, locating it in the lower element of the body, and assigning the fallibility of the flesh primarily to the female gender (Miles, 2013: 141–2).

1.1 Bodily Existence in the New Testament

This development happened over some time. The pages of the New Testament, perhaps more than the writings of the early Church fathers, members of a classically educated literate elite, give some indication of ordinary Christian belief and practice, although highly redacted by literate members of the community, from the mid-first century to approximately the late second. Here we see Christian teachers, as the end of the present age and the return of Christ recede further into the future, having to deal with the bodily here-and-now but also with the continuing anticipation of a bodily resurrection, however far in the future. Paul's writings especially wrestle with defining "body" and its struggle between the competing realms of spirit and of flesh. In Galatians, Paul treats flesh versus spirit as an aspect of anti-circumcision (for Gentiles), but he does not limit it to that: "If you sow in your flesh, you will reap corruption from the flesh, but if you sow from the spirit, you will reap eternal life from the spirit" (Gal 6:7).[5] He also expresses a belief that would become highly influential in martyrologies: "I carry the marks of Jesus branded on my body," as if on the body of a slave (Gal 6:17). The fleshly mark of belonging to God was for him no longer circumcision, but the imprint of service, persecution, and self-denial. Paul again uses the conflict of flesh versus spirit in his letter to the Romans: "I see in my members another law at war with the law of my mind, making me captive to the law of sin that dwells in my [bodily] members. Wretched man that I am! Who will rescue me from this body of death?" (Rom 7:23–4).

---

[5] All scriptural quotations in English, unless otherwise noted, are from the New Revised Standard Version.

Paul continues to set flesh against spirit: "For those who live according to the flesh set their minds on the things of the flesh, but those who live according to the Spirit set their minds on the things of the Spirit" (Rom 8:5–6).[6]

The letter to the Colossians, whose authorship by Paul is disputed, does not emphasize the conflict of spirit versus flesh so much as it does the victory through bodily suffering of the witness to Christ: "I am now rejoicing in my sufferings for your sake, and in my flesh. I am completing what is lacking in Christ's afflictions for the sake of his body: that is, the church" (Col 1:24). Christ's own body was the vehicle for the "indwelling" of the Deity (2:9). Similarly, in 2 Corinthians, Paul distinguishes his authentic apostolic authority from that of the would-be "hyper-apostles" because he and his companions are "always carrying in the body the death of Jesus, so that the life of Jesus may also be visible in our bodies" (2 Cor 4:10).

1.2 Body Metaphors in the Corinthian Correspondence

The Corinthian correspondence gives us Paul's most memorable use of body as metaphor. It is a metaphor for unity: the newly baptized become part of an actual new creation or foundation (*ktisis*; 1 Cor 5:17), the church as the body of Christ: "For just as the body is one and has many members, and all the members of the body, though many, are one body, so it is with Christ. For in the one Spirit we were all baptized into one body . . . and we were all made to drink of one Spirit" (1 Cor 12:13). Here, body and spirit have no conflict and together symbolize the unity of the "body of Christ," the church, in which the spirit dwells (12:27). Paul continues to emphasize bodies, both actual and metaphorical, in two ways: first, through the importance of sexual self-control in Chapter 7, which is later to become a major influence on norms of ascetic behavior; and second, in his discourse on resurrection in Chapter 15. In the first, Paul acknowledges but does not endorse marriage: for him, it is a stopgap for sexual immorality and lack of self-control (7:2–9). Far better, he thinks, is to "be anxious about the affairs of the Lord" rather than to be anxious for worldly things like pleasing one's spouse (7:12–13). Paul offers an athletic training metaphor (*askēsis*) for earthly life, one that he delineates

[6] See also Jn 3:6.

more fully in 9:26–7: "So I do not run aimlessly, nor do I box as though beating the air, but I punish my body and enslave it." Here, he seems to imply a distinct mind/body hierarchy, in which the body (here, the realm dominated by flesh) should be a slave, disciplined by the mind.

In Chapter 15, Paul addresses the problem that the Gentiles in his audience had with the Jewish idea of the resurrection of the body: clearly, when one dies (however one dies), it is the physical body, allied to the flesh, that dies. How can that be raised? Paul envisions a spiritual "body" that involves the transformation of the human entity: "It is sown a physical body, it is raised a spiritual body. If there is a physical body, there is also a spiritual body" (15:44). Otherwise, Paul believes, the resurrection of Jesus, whose incarnation and crucifixion are foundational for his faith, makes no sense. This idea of the transformation of the transitory physical body into the eternal resurrected body plays a great role in the stories of the martyrs, as we will see in Section 4.1 with the afterlives of Perpetua and Saturus in the *Martyrdom of Perpetua and Felicitas* (11:2; 12:27; 13:4).

1.3 The Discipleship of Equals

Although Paul initially may seem to have advocated a "discipleship of equals," in Elisabeth Schüssler Fiorenza's (1983: 95) phrase, claiming that "in Christ" differences such as male and female do not prevail (Gal 3:27–8); nevertheless, as Christianity departs from its radical roots and comes closer to conformity with "this world," the divide between women's and men's physical bodies persists in this life, if not in the resurrection. Despite Jesus' saying that "In the resurrection, they neither marry nor are given in marriage, but are like angels in heaven" (Matt 22:30), later letters like the Deutero-Pauline, Pastoral, and Catholic Epistles, which are concerned more with taking the existing world as it is and transforming it in a Christian direction, characterize women who reject marriage as "silly" and "overwhelmed by their sins, and swayed by all kinds of desires" (1 Tim 3:6–7); subject to their passions (Tit 3:3); and also as the "weaker sex" (1 Pet 3:7). A wife can even be considered the "body" belonging to her husband (Eph 5:28). Similarly, slaves, whose bodies were at the disposal of their owners, especially female slaves, who were the "reproductive bodies" of their masters (Glancy, 2002: 11), were enjoined to be obedient (Eph 6:5–8; Col 3:22–4; Tit 9–10) and even to endure being beaten because Christ also suffered (1 Pet 2:18–25). Suffering is a form of imitation of Christ.

2 Equal Opportunity: Martyrs and Ascetics

There were nonetheless two realms in which men and women, slave and free, were truly equal or, rather, one in which women became men and were therefore equal to them: martyrdom and the ascetic life. In the first part of what follows, on the subject of early Christian martyrdom, I will examine a selection of martyrologies, focusing on those collected by Herbert Musurillo (1972), the hagiographies from the Apocryphal Acts of the Apostles (J. K. Elliott,1993), and Palladius' *Lausiac History* (Clarke, 1918), together with Brock and Harvey's (1987) *Holy Women of the Syrian Orient*. I will not attempt to examine whether or not some or all of the martyrologies are "authentic": Allison Elliott (1988: 25) claims that "seventy authentic *passiones* survive." Moss (2013: 18) considers far fewer authentic or historical: she holds that six "can be treated as reliable": the *Martyrdom of Polycarp*, the *Martyrdom of Perpetua and Felicitas*, the *Apologies* of Justin Martyr, the *Acts of the Scillitan Martyrs* (which will not concern us here) and the *Martyrs of Lyons and Vienne*, as recorded by Eusebius in his *History of the Church*. Nonetheless, the point is not the historicity or reliability of these martyr accounts. As L. Stephanie Cobb notes, these texts are never meant to be history but to be "rhetorically effective" and "religiously instructive" (Cobb, 2016: 9). With regard to their depiction of women, Ross Kraemer offers the caveat that we need to attend "far more carefully to the degree to which the rhetorical uses of gender obscure our version of antiquity" (Kraemer, 2011: 11).

2.1 Martyrologies and Hagiographies as Propaganda for the Virtues

Martyrologies, like hagiographies – the stories of ascetic holy men and women – provide examples for Christian behavior and model definitions of Christian identity, not only as they adopt and modify accepted Greco-Roman definitions of virtue but also as they add specific Christian virtues to the list, virtues that imitate, surpass, and ultimately replace Roman public, as well as private, virtues. These virtues (for men) include *parrhēsia* (the open speech of free citizen males), which is often eschewed rather than embraced by women, in favor of imitating the silence of Jesus during his ordeal. Only in the gospel of John does Jesus have any extended speech: otherwise, as the evangelist Luke indicates, his silence is that of the sacrificial lamb (Acts 8:30–55, quoting Isa 53:7–8). In martyrdoms, moreover, actual speech is not necessary: like the body of Jesus, the bodies of the martyrs embody speech. Their public *martyria* (witness) in the arena becomes a form of free and open speech even more potent than their spoken responses at their trials.

One of the most important, maybe even central virtues in these accounts is *andreia* (Greek) or *virtus* (Latin), both of which literally mean "manliness" but are usually translated as "courage." Courage or fortitude is one of Stoic philosophy's cardinal or governing virtues, together with *sōphrosynē*, self-control, or in its more severe form, *enkrateia*, self-mastery (Cicero, *On Invention*, 2.53; Cobb, 2008: 6–8; Cooper, 1996: 17). Women's virtues are more often characterized by the private qualities of modesty and chastity. But in the arena, women could also imitate and often surpass the primary male virtue of *andreia*, effectively becoming men (Cobb, 2008: 5; Streete, 2018: 41). Yet private female virtues could also be publicly displayed: Perpetua demands that she and Felicitas not be exposed naked in the arena (although she has no problem being naked as a male gladiator in one of her visions, M*artyrdom*, 10.7), and she even straightens her torn dress and pins up her disheveled hair when she is tossed by the mad heifer, "more mindful of shame (*pudor*, modesty) than of pain (*dolor*)," as the narrator in the Latin version of the *Martyrdom* puns (20:4–5). Susan Hylen (2015: 119), who calls Thecla a "modest" apostle, demonstrates that there was a "complexity" in both Roman and Christian norms of modesty that did not necessarily make women passively obedient but might also be willingly embraced by them as a marker of Christian identity. In the less public, but still visible, arena of ascetic practice, women also became men by exercising *sōphrosynē* and *enkrateia*, often adopting male dress and living as men. Stories of "harlot saints" who chose this route as a form of penitence abound, as will later be shown in Section 3.5. For the most part, however, the main virtue of the female martyr is *andreia*, the public virtue by which she becomes a man; the main virtue of the female ascetic is *enkrateia*, another prime masculine virtue, which entails mastering the passions and controlling sexual desire and its expression. Both virtues are complementary rather than separable or exclusive.

2.2 Martyrdom and Christian Identity

Christians as an entity, although not always under that name, made their first appearance in the writings of Roman historians of the second century CE. Suetonius (69–122) mentions an expulsion of Jews from Rome by the emperor Claudius (41–54) in 49 CE, because of riots *impulsore Chresto*, "at the instigation of [one] Chrestus" (*Claudius*, 25), which has often been taken to refer to disputes between Jewish sects, including the upstart followers of Jesus. "Chrestus," however, is a fairly common slave name, and the expulsion may have occurred because of Roman fears of another slave uprising like that of Spartacus and his allies in 73 BCE. Suetonius also commends the emperor Nero (*Nero*, 16) for regulating several organized groups, including his "punishment inflicted on the Christians, a class of men given to a mischievous superstition." This punishment is briefly mentioned by Suetonius before he passes on to Nero's regulation of chariot drivers: he seems to treat both equally and to approve of both as contributing to the Roman order.

The Roman historian Tacitus (56–120) describes this punishment of Christians in greater detail in his *Annals* 15.44–5. In his account, the emperor Nero was suspected of having started the Great Fire of Rome in 64 but cleverly "fastened the guilt and inflicted the most exquisite tortures on a class hated for their abominations, called Christians by the populace." Tacitus goes on to trace the "most mischievous superstition" to its origin with "Christus," who "suffered the extreme penalty during the reign of Tiberius at the hands of one of our procurators, Pontius Pilatus." Tacitus relates how those who pleaded guilty (presumably after torture) gave information that convicted a "multitude," not so much because of the fire but their hatred of mankind." He describes the spectacle of their punishment in the Circus Maximus as including "mockery of every sort," in which

Christians were "covered with the skins of beasts," set upon by dogs, crucified, or burned alive as human torches at night, when Nero "offered his gardens for the spectacle," driving around dressed as a charioteer. Tacitus has no sympathy for those Christian "criminals," who "deserved extreme and exemplary punishment," but he reluctantly admits that a "feeling of compassion" arose from the populace, because Christians were not being executed "for the public good" but "to glut one man's cruelty," an example of the disdain this senatorial aristocrat felt for the gauche emperor.

Tacitus' friend, the younger Pliny, governor of the Roman province of Bithynia and Pontus, sheds further light on the early relationship of Christians to the Roman imperial administration. Pliny writes to the emperor Trajan for advice on how to conduct examinations and trials of those who have been accused of being "Christian" (Pliny, *Letters*, 10.96). He informs the emperor of his procedures and looks for approval of his conduct. When Christians are arrested, they are asked three times if they are Christian, have been Christian, or have given it up. He wonders whether he should apply torture to anyone accused of being Christian (thus assuming they are not citizens or have forfeited their right to be so), regardless of age, gender, or "bodily weakness." He says that he has already questioned under torture – standard Roman legal procedure – two slave women (*ancillae*) who are called *ministrae*, ministers, presumably functionaries in the Christian community. He found nothing other than "a depraved and excessive superstition" that seems not to pose a real threat to Rome, "superstition" designating any practice that is not legally sanctioned by the Roman definition of religion, as a public affair that supported the state. Pliny says that he has accordingly executed those who persist in their Christianity because of their "obstinacy" and "stubbornness." Trajan replies as an "enlightened" and modern emperor that Pliny's procedure is correct, but Christians are not to be hunted down, neither are anonymous accusations to be credited.

This exchange of letters provides a model for the stories of Christian martyrdoms; although, as the correspondence indicates, for much of the first three centuries of Christian development, there was little organized persecution. When it did occur, it was sporadic, even during the three empire-wide proscriptions against the Christians: in 250 (Decius), in 257–8 (Valerian), and in 303–11 (Diocletian, Galerius, and Maximinus) (Moss, 2013: 233). Those accused of practicing the non-sanctioned religion or superstition known as Christianity were brought to a public trial before a Roman official. There, they were given the opportunity to offer their *martyria*, their testimony in their defense against the criminal charge of subverting the Roman peace by practicing *asebeia*, or disrespect of the gods (atheism). As Margo Kitts has noted, the concept of *martyria* as "witness" or "testimony" had changed by the first century CE, especially in the New Testament, from the idea of a divine spectator invoked to punish violators of oaths, accompanied by a ritual slaughter of animals, with their supposed willingness to die and an emphasis on their suffering, to "the victim who suffers and dies in testimony to a perceived truth" (Kitts, 2018: 77). Spectacle and suffering have thus become essential elements of martyrdom.

In Christian martyrdoms, the accused often refuse even to give their actual names, preferring instead to be known by the name of "Christian." Perpetua claims that she cannot be called by any other name than that of Christian: "*Christiana sum*" (*Martyrdom of Perpetua and Felicitas*, 3.2). In the *Martyrdom of Saints Carpus, Papylus, and Agathonike*, from the late second century CE, Carpus, although crying and screaming under torture, keeps claiming, "I am a Christian" (23). In the account of the *Martyrs of Lyons and Vienne* (Eusebius, *HE* 18–19), even when her "entire body was broken and torn," Blandina admits, "I am a Christian, and we do nothing to be ashamed of." The soldier Maximilian (*Acts of Maximilian*, 2) refuses to give a name other than "Christian," while Dasius, also a soldier, simply gives the name "Christian" (*Martyrdom of the Holy Dasius*, 8), and Euplus acknowledges the fate his confession will bring him: "I want to die; I am a Christian" (*Acts of Euplus*, 1).

These martyrs also disavow earthly family ties and connections in favor of this new eschatological identity of Christian, as they believed Jesus had taught them (Lk 14:26–7). Perpetua rejects her father; her husband is nowhere in the picture; and eventually she has to give up her infant son, who was a source of concern to her in the prison. Felicitas gives her prematurely born baby girl to be raised by a Christian "sister." Papylus, a Roman citizen, claims that he has "many children," but only in the faith.

Agathonike, when urged to "Have pity on your son" (44), and in the Latin version, to "have pity on your children," says only that "God will pity" them (6).

The trial of these Christians, and their subsequent condemnation to execution, which takes various forms depending on their social rank, provides a public forum for the Christian witness, in both speech and act. It also provides a space for the demonstration of identity with Christ and for the particularly Christian virtues of humility (Gk. *tapeinōsis*, Lat. *humilitas*) and patient endurance (*hypomonē*). The suffering and "humiliating" deaths of the martyrs transform them into "consecrated warriors" and noble athletes, male and female alike (Kitts, 2018: 276–7). Christ is of course the supreme sacrificial victim, whose body and blood were celebrated in one of the earliest of Christian rituals, the Eucharist (1 Cor 11:23–6). He is also the exemplar of the Christian virtues of humility and *hypomonē*, as demonstrated in Paul's letter to the Philippians 2:6–11, virtues that his followers were urged to imitate. Christ "emptied" his being of divinity, taking on the "form of a slave," enduring even death on a cross, for which God has "exalted him." The letter to the Hebrews mentions a "great cloud of witnesses (*martyres*)" to the faith, including not only the patriarchs and prophets but also the unlikely "Rahab the prostitute" (11:29; Josh 2.1–21, 6:22–5). The "pioneer and perfecter" of their faith is Jesus, who "endured (*hypemeinen*) the cross." The same *hypomonē* should be demonstrated by his followers as imitators (Heb 12:1–2).

The deaths of Jesus' followers and confessors at the hands of their opponents, the imperial Roman authorities, were also redemptive, not only of the martyrs themselves but also of others. The redemptive quality of martyrdom appears in the Hellenistic Jewish apocryphal work from the second century CE,[7] 4 Maccabees, especially in 12:11–17, where the martyrs are guaranteed eternal life with God and the patriarchs, avoiding the torment of those who deny God. The early account of the death of the first Christian martyr Stephen in Acts 7 mentions that he sees just before his death "the heavens opened, and the Son of Man standing at the right hand of

---

[7] The actual date of composition is uncertain.

God!" (Acts 7:56). The gospel of Luke, by the same author as that of the book of Acts, relates the story of the repentant thief who confesses to Jesus as the messiah and is promised entrance into Paradise "today" (Lk 23:42–3). The first epistle of Peter (1 Pet 4:1) is quite specific about the redemptive quality of Christian suffering: "Since, therefore, Christ suffering in the flesh, arm yourselves also with the same intention (for whoever has suffered in the flesh has finished with sin)." Martyrs, and even confessors, those who are imprisoned for their faith but have not died for it, are also believed to have the power to atone for the sins of others. The slave Blandina is hung on a post in the arena "in the form of a cross," silently encouraging her fellow martyrs in their ordeal as they see "in the person of their sister him who was crucified for them" (*Martyrs of Lyons and Vienne*, 74). Imprisoned for her faith, the noble Perpetua is granted the power of prophetic vision and also of intercession for her dead brother Dinocrates, who is suffering in a "dark place" (*Martyrdom of Perpetua and Felicitas*, 4.1). The same narrative relates a vision of the martyr Saturus, in which he and Perpetua are called from heaven to intercede between Optatus the bishop and Aspasius the presbyter (13.4). Thecla, about to be martyred by the beasts in Antioch, is urged by her protector Tryphaina to intercede for her dead daughter, Falconilla, so that she may be translated to "the place of the just" (*Acts of Paul and Thecla*, 28).

2.3 Christian Bodily Witness (Martyria) as Propaganda

In the last book of the New Testament, Revelation, one's identity as a Christian depends exclusively on one's willingness to become a martyr, "a faithful witness to the truth" (Rev 3:14; Kitts, 2018: 275–6). Indeed, the author of the book, who identifies himself as John, shares with his audience his own "persecution and the kingdom and the patient endurance [*hypomonē*]" and claims to be on the island of Patmos "because of the word of God and the testimony [*martyria*] of [or to] Jesus" (1:9). Martyrdom as depicted in this book means not only verbal testimony but also willingness to suffer and die for this witness, with no compromise with those who are allies of the Great Whore: namely, the Roman Empire (2:13; 19:10; 20:4). The reward of those who have died for their faith is to "conquer" their enemies by paradoxically enduring suffering at their hands, in loyalty to a superior empire, the Kingdom of God. Following the model of the Book of Revelation, martyr account after martyr account shares this language of conquest, as if the martyrs are soldiers in battle or noble athletes in a contest, fighters in the arena, rather than despised *noxii*, criminals accused of trying to overthrow the Roman state by their stubborn refusal to participate in its religiopolitical rituals (Kyle, 1998: 91). As Elizabeth Castelli (2000: 197) notes, "The discourse of martyrdom is a discourse of power," but it is a paradoxical power that is acquired by those who have little or no earthly power or authority, "a strength made perfect in weakness," as Paul claims for himself in 2 Cor 12:9. God (or God in Christ) becomes the ally of the weak and powerless, including women and slaves, to defeat the powers of this world, just as in the accounts of the ascetic holy people, as will be shown in Section 3.4, the power of bodily self-control and dedication to God defeats the demons.

Martyrologies as propaganda for encouragement and exhortation take two approaches. In the first, the apologetic approach, the martyrologist attempts to show, as we have previously noted, that Christians are not, as the Roman authorities think them, subversives of the state; they subscribe to the same virtues as do other Romans and, in fact, are better at demonstrating them. Christian martyrs "embraced, rather than replaced, Roman definitions of honor, strength, and reason" (Cobb, 2008: 2) and in doing so transformed them. In the second approach, the martyrologist enlists the sympathy of the readers/hearers to inspire them, if not to imitation, at least to admiration.[8] Justin Martyr (110–165), who has the unique position of being Christianity's first philosopher/apologist/martyr, asserts that Christians serve God "rationally," as true philosophers (*First Apology*, 13).[9] He responds to a possible charge that if the Christians believe they

---

[8] Augustine (*Sermon* 280.1.1) on the *dies natalis* (literally, "birthday," but actually the date of martyrdom) of Perpetua and Felicitas, says that men (*viri*) may "more admire than imitate them." Rubén Rosario Rodriguez (2017: 259) suggests that the purpose of the martyrs' witness is nonviolent social resistance, a precursor to liberation theology.

[9] The Stoic-leaning author of 4 Maccabees similarly represents Judaism as the "true philosophy," one that is worth dying for, and one that teaches a noble death.

must resist the state, an act that makes them criminals, why not perform a "noble death" by suicide rather than risking a horrible death in the arena? Justin's answer is that without the public witness, the "speaking the martyrdom" (Boyarin, 1999: 94–5; A. Elliott, 1988: 24–5), their death is meaningless: "If, then, we all kill ourselves we shall become the cause, as far as in us lies, why no one should be ... instructed in the divine doctrines" (*Second Apology*, 4). Tertullian, more flamboyantly, asserts, "the blood of the Christians is seed" (*Apologetic*, 50).

Although we do have the early *martyria* of Justin and his fellow Christians (*Acts of Justin and Companions*), one of the most important testimonies to the way in which literate, elite Christians thought of their possible "dying for God" is that attributed to the Syrian bishop Ignatius of Antioch, who supposedly died sometime within the reign of the "enlightened" emperor, Trajan. In a letter to the Roman Christians at the center of the empire, Ignatius, arrested because of his status as a bishop and leader of other Christians, as was often the case, writes that Christians should not prevent or oppose his martyrdom because of their "carnal affection" for him. Instead, he envisions his body as being transformed into something very different:

> Suffer me to become food for wild beasts. . . . I am the wheat
> of God and am ground by the teeth of the wild beasts, that
> I may be found the pure bread of God. . . . May they leave
> nothing of my body. . . . Then shall I be a true disciple of
> Jesus Christ, when the world shall not see so much as my
> body. (To the Romans, 4)

He continues, "Let fire and the cross; let the crowds of wild beasts, let tearings, breakings, and dislocations of bones; let cutting off of members, let shatterings of the whole body; and let all dreadful torments of the devil come upon me: only let me attain to Jesus Christ" (*To the Romans*, 5). Ignatius' perfervid imagination of his own martyrdom is significant because he sees his body as transformed into Christ's body (as Eucharistic bread), and thence into a fleshless *persona* (Streete, 2009: 18). Even so, Ignatius' insistent wishes emphasize his body as central to his *martyria* (Streete, 2018:

46). This is a male body that he envisions dissolving; although he does not stress the masculinity of his body, he uses language that suggests appropriately "masculine" behavior under bodily trial: the *andreia* or *virtus* (courage) that is the quality of being a man but that is also being defined as the Christian *hypomonē* (endurance) – especially of extreme pain. Indeed, as Cobb (2008: 2–3) remarks, "The stories of the martyrs depict Christians as more masculine – a principal Roman attribute – than non-Christians. . . . To be a Christian was to embody masculinity."

Another martyrology in the form of a letter, perhaps modeled on that of Ignatius, that uses the same themes of masculine bravery and endurance of pain is the *Martyrdom of Polycarp*, who was bishop of Smyrna from 120 to 140 CE. The virtue of *hypomonē* is present throughout the narrative (e.g., 2.2, 2.3, 13), as is the theme of the imitation of Christ (1.2; Moss, 2010: 46–7). The young martyr who precedes Polycarp, Germanicus, is described as "most noble" (*Martyrdom of Polycarp*, 3.3), because, being urged by the governor who is presiding at his trial to "spare his young manhood," he instead bravely pulls the beast who is attacking him more forcefully on top of him (3.1).[10] A counterexample is that of Quintus, who gave himself up voluntarily and urged others to do the same; however, on seeing the beasts he "turned cowardly" and thus became unmanly and recanted (4). Polycarp, now a very old man, sees in a vision that "It is necessary that I be burnt alive" (5). As he enters the arena, he hears a voice saying, "Be strong, Polycarp, and *andrizou*," usually translated as "Be the man." (In modern parlance it would be "Man up.") He thus refuses to recant, takes off all his clothing, and faces the fire naked.[11] Polycarp's body is thence

[10] This action recalls that of Thecla, who leaps into the pit of seals prepared for her death, claiming that she is "baptized on the last day!" (*Acts of Paul and Thecla*, 34).

[11] Nakedness in martyrdoms has different meanings. For men, it symbolizes stripping for combat, for the *agon* or contest in the arena. When Pionius (*Martyrdom of Pionius*, Musurillo, 1972) is nailed up, he is naked, so that the "holiness" and "beauty" of his body are visible (21). For women, nakedness is a mark of shame, although Perpetua in one of her dreams strips naked when she becomes a male gladiator.

transformed into something other than human: he is a "noble ram from
a great flock," a "holocaust," and a "sacrifice" (14), hoping for the resurrection of the "soul and the body," again recalling the atoning death and
resurrection of Christ. His death on the pyre is described as a "wonder": his
flesh is "not as burning flesh," but as "bread being baked" (a possible
reference to the Eucharistic body of Christ) or "like gold and silver being
purified," giving forth a "delightful fragrance" like "costly perfume" (15).
His body is transformed but not consumed by the fire, and so a dagger is
plunged into his body: the blood quenches the flames. In this way, Polycarp
wins "an incontestable prize," and his remains are "dearer than precious
stones and finer than gold" (17–18). By his endurance, Polycarp's body is
transformed into something more than earthly, sacrificed, like that of Jesus,
on behalf of others, and even remains on earth in some form as relics to
encourage his followers.

2.4 Women Acting Like Men

In the *Martyrdom of Saint Justin and Companions*, all confess before the
prefect Urbicus that they are Christian, confident that even when they are
scourged and beheaded (a death indicating their higher social status),
they will "ascend to heaven" (5). In one version of this text, the presiding
magistrate marks one of their number, Charito (or Charites), for special
questioning: "What is this, woman? Have you been deceived by their
words? You do not, at any rate, present a good reputation," presumably
because she ought, because of her rank, to have more sense and modesty
than to be found in such criminal company. She replies, "I am not
deceived. . . . Rather, I have become God's servant and a Christian and
by his power I have kept myself free from the taints of the flesh" (3).
Charito thus implies that purity of the flesh (chastity) is an essential part
of being a female martyr, a theme that we shall find elsewhere, particularly in the *Acts of Paul and Thecla* and its variants, which blend
martyrdom and asceticism into a single martyrology. Other martyr
texts, like those recounted by Brock and Harvey (1987), also use
a woman's choice of the virginal or celibate life as the reason for her
martyrdom, a theme that will be explored in the discussion of asceticism
in Section 3.1.

One of the most important and most cited of early Christian martyrologies is the third-century *Martyrdom of Perpetua and Felicitas*. Musurillo (1972: 56–7) even claims that it is a model for all subsequent martyr texts. Long considered a part of a "lost tradition" and resurrected in the 1980s with the intention to recover women's religious histories, there is no current discussion of martyrdoms or women's roles in them without this text, which is remarkable largely because it contains what purports to be the prison diary of Perpetua herself, including an account of four visions, although the actual martyrdom and the introduction and addition of passages about the deacon Saturus, his visions, and his martyrdom, are clearly by a different hand (Wilson-Kastner et al., 1981: 1–32). Perpetua is described as *honeste nata*, or born into a relatively high social class, and educated (*Martyrdom of Perpetua and Felicitas*, 2.1). In this respect, she is unlike the slave Felicitas, who is a "usable" (and therefore exploitable) body, subject to the sexual predilections of a master" (Streete, 2009: 40), and so no one would expect her to be treated the same as her fellow Christians. But for Perpetua, as for all Christians in the martyr texts, her identity as a Christian supersedes her identity as a member of a privileged Roman social class, and she refuses to renounce it, even though her father, at the urging of the governor who presides at her trial, makes several attempts to persuade her to do so. Although she claims other privileges, such as better treatment in prison, they are for her brother and sister Christians and not solely for herself. Torture, for example, seems remarkably absent in this account, except perhaps for Felicitas' suffering during the delivery of a premature baby (15:6–7).

One reason this martyrdom has been so remarkable to later commentators is that it demonstrates the unique position of the female martyr. If, as Cobb (2008: 3) claims, Christianity was the "embodiment of masculinity," then women needed to demonstrate a masculine identity, but at the same time to "exemplify female virtues" (Cobb: 2008: 8). The courage that was also manliness exhibited by the martyr in the arena was thus doubly emphasized in the case of women, whose supposed mental and bodily weakness would make them incapable of such endurance. Instead, these women, who, as Augustine remarked, were easier for *men* (*viri*) to admire than imitate (*Sermon* 1.1), in a sense "overcame" their female minds and bodies even as they battled their opponents to become heroic, "noble athletes," just as the torn and broken Blandina becomes in her suffering (*Martyrs of Lyons and Vienne*, 5.1.41; B. Shaw, 1996: 300). In one of her remarkable visions in prison, Perpetua actually becomes a male athlete, stripped for combat in the arena: "My clothes were stripped off, and I became a man" (*Martyrdom of Perpetua and Felicitas*, 10.7). Ironically, however, to show women acting as men, it is necessary for a martyrology to present them visually as female. Felicitas, whose prayer to give birth to a premature daughter so that she could suffer with her fellow martyrs is answered, goes into hard labor and is taunted in her pain (15.6). Perpetua and Felicitas, at first stripped naked for the arena before being re-clothed, are pointedly called *puellae* (girls) in the text, while even the crowd is appalled by their appearance: one a "delicate girl" (Perpetua) and the other a mother "with dripping breasts," who has recently given birth (Felicitas). When tossed with a "mad heifer," which is "matched to her sex" (20.1), Perpetua's first thoughts are to fasten up her hair and fix her torn dress (20.4), a sign of her feminine modesty and sense of shame, as previously noted. She even dies in the classic gesture of feminine suicide (Loraux, 1985: 3), guiding the trembling hand of the young soldier who is assigned to kill her to her throat, as the narrator exclaims, "So great a woman!"

The *Acta Martyrum*, Acts of the Christian Martyrs, are rife with stories of female martyrs whose bodies are displayed for spectators to gaze upon, as they demonstrate both their physical femaleness and their male courage: the one reinforces the other. In one version of the *Martyrdom of Saints Carpus, Papylus, and Agathonike*, Agathonike voluntarily takes off all of her clothes, stripping as if for a gladiatorial combat. While the crowd of spectators, seeing her beauty, grieves for its destruction in her forthcoming death, she "throws herself on the pyre" (51). The body of Blandina, in the *Martyrs of Lyons and Vienne*, is "exposed" as she is hung on a cross; the perfection of Potimiaena's body is mentioned as she is about to be raped by gladiators (*Martyrdom of Potimiaena and Basilides*, 74–5). Irene (*Martyrdom of Agape, Chione, and Irene*) is ordered to be "placed naked in a brothel" unless she recants. Crispina (*Martyrdom of Crispina*) is ordered to have her head shaved by the proconsul Anullinus (304–5), a form of public shame for women (e.g., 1 Cor 11:5), to achieve her "complete disfigurement." Thecla, in the *Acts of Paul and Thecla*, is displayed naked on a number of occasions: when she is to be burned in Iconium as a "lawless one," when she is thrown to the seals in Antioch, and when she is assaulted by the beasts in the arena in Antioch. As Gilbert Dagron (1978: 26), observes, she is "depicted naked more often than usual." In their accounts of the holy women of the Syrian Orient, Brock and Harvey (1987) draw many examples of women – Anahid, Ruhm, Elizabeth the deaconess, Mahya, and Febronia, among others – who are sexually as well as physically mutilated because they are women:

> The sexual mutilation of women by torture and the sexual annihilation of women by taking on of a male identity [as in the example of ascetic women] are both about the same issue – namely, power and dominance in the relationship between men and women. And these events are found in hagiography about women, both legendary and historical. . . . What are we to hear? (Brock and Harvey, 1987: 25)

Perhaps one of the things their audience is intended to hear is the extraordinary resilience of a body that is devoted to God. As Cobb (2016: 9) notes, martyr texts were read and heard on the *dies natalis*, the anniversary of the martyr's death and so their "birthday" into eternal life, in liturgical contexts in churches or at the shrine of the martyr, as the late fourth-century pilgrim Egeria recounts happening at Thecla's *martyrium* in Seleucia (Wilson-Kastner et al., 1981: 74–83), to "bring the miraculous deeds of God into the present" (Cobb, 2016: 157). The martyrs may be mutilated, but most texts depict them as not suffering, as defiant, even as healed from their wounds. The body of Anahid, for example, is said to be "without a scar," after graphically depicted extreme torture, disfigurement, and captivity (Brock and Harvey, 1987: 94). Cobb suggests that martyr texts like these imply that the Christian faith offers a remedy for the universal human condition: "a life of pain" (Cobb, 2016: 157). Female martyrs are especially notable in this respect because, as the text of Blandina's martyr-dom shows, despite the feared "bodily weakness" of a female and a slave at that, she is "filled with such power" that her torturers become exhausted

(*Martyrs of Lyons and Vienne*, 18). More importantly, her endurance of torture and the "exercises" or "combats" (*gymnasmata*) in the arena made

> irreversible the condemnation of the crooked serpent [who had deceived Eve], and, tiny, weak, and insignificant as she was, she would give inspiration to her brothers [male Christians], for she had put on Christ, that mighty and invincible athlete, and had overcome the Adversary in many contests, and through her conflict (*agōn*) had won the crown of immortality. (36)

3 Martyrdom as Asceticism: Thecla and the Apocryphal Acts of the Apostles

> With the Peace of Constantine in 313 . . . the days of literal martyrdom largely came to an end.[12] The successors of the martyrs were the desert fathers [and mothers], those heroes of self-persecution who fled the cities for . . . the uninhabited deserts of Egypt, Syria, and Palestine. But if the goal of these spiritual martyrs was the same as that of their predecessors, the kingdom of heaven, the hermits' methods of attaining it differed. . . . The *vita* of the confessor saint stands in the same relationship to the *passio* as romance does to epic. The enemy is now within – the Devil himself and not his public representative or surrogate, the Roman magistrate. (A. Elliott, 1988: 42)

[12] Voluntary martyrdom at the hands of an increasingly orthodox Christian empire, however, continued to be sought, particularly by North African Christians like the Donatists and related groups, who believed that the willingness to be martyred was the mark of a true Christian, and sacraments administered by Christian clergy who had shunned martyrdom by the Roman Empire were invalid. Brock and Harvey (1987) recount martyrdoms and persecutions of Christians in the Syrian Orient attributed to Jews, Zoroastrians, and Chalcedonian (orthodox) Christians well into the sixth century.

The physical and mental training and discipline required for endurance in the contests of the arena carried over as the foundation for continued demonstrations of Christian *sōphrosynē*, the self-control and subduing of the flesh that stubbornly remained a part of this world, even though the world's end was continually expected. Christian male leaders, the church fathers, "frequently asserted that asceticism was a new form of martyrdom, one in which we could be martyred daily" (Clark, 1986: 45). The Christian athletes contending in the arena were still praised for their "conquests," but the arena had changed. Yet, in the Apocryphal Acts of the Apostles, which are some of the primary documents for the promotion of this continued combat of flesh *versus* spirit, the literal arena persists. This is the case with the *Acts of Paul and Thecla* in which a "noble virgin" of Iconium (much like the well-born matron Perpetua) is faced in several instances with physical trials in public arenas. The *Acts of Thecla*, a lengthy second-century episode embedded in the *Apocryphal Acts of Paul*, known collectively as the *Acts of Paul and Thecla* (McLarty, 2018: 3), belongs to a genre of what can only be called Christian "anti-romances," modeled on the so-called "Greek romance," "chastity romance," or "romance novel" (Hennecke and Schneemelcher, II, 1964–5: 32), in which a young noble couple fall in love but are separated and have to undergo a series of adventures and trials that test their fidelity, and particularly the woman's chastity. As Peter Brown (1988: 14) observes, "The novels ... explored with a new respect the theme of love at first sight among the young. Both hero and heroine were presented as passing through dramatic trials to preserve their chastity for a predestinate marriage." In the end, however, they are reunited, with the woman's chastity intact, to initiate (or resume) a married life together.

Kate Cooper (1996: 27) notes that these novels also show that love (desire) is "not in tension with the social order" but rather contributes to it, since marriage is the foundation of stable civic life. Several commentators, like D. MacDonald (1985) and Burrus (1987), have observed that the Christian Apocryphal Acts of the Apostles adopt this novelistic pattern, but, as in the martyr texts that employ the rhetoric of Roman virtues only to show how much better Christians are at them than non-Christians, these Acts adopt the rhetoric of chastity and continence to subvert the marriage plot and to advocate for lifelong celibacy: "The impulse of the [Greek romance] texts is deeply conservative, social rather than anti-social; their Christian transformations are far from it" (Cooper, 1996: 37).

One of the best examples of this transformation/subversion is the *Acts of Paul and Thecla*. In the part of these Acts that describes her actions, Thecla, a noble virgin of Iconium, while she is still enclosed in her house, as a chaste unmarried woman should be, listens from her window, the precarious liminal space between her home and the outside, to "the word of the celibate life" as spoken by Paul, in the neighboring house of Onesiphorus (*Acts of Paul and Thecla*, 7). His voice enchants her, although Paul himself is depicted as a scarcely erotic object in his physical appearance: "small in size, bald-headed, bandy-legged ... with eyebrows meeting, rather hook-nosed" (3). Perhaps his attraction is spiritual: he is also described as "noble in mien," and sometimes "had the face of an angel." Troubled, because her daughter will not move from her post, fearing that she is attracted by a "new and terrible passion" (9), Thecla's mother Theocleia calls for her fiancé, Thamyris, to summon her back to her civic responsibilities and her social role therein. But like the martyrs who precede her, Thecla is "dead" to her mother, her fiancé, and above all to her household: even the maids mourn for her (10). Shamelessly, Thecla leaves her house and seeks Paul in prison, where she kisses his chains and rolls on the ground where he sat. Ironically and paradoxically, these actions are not portrayed as erotic in the strictly physical sense, but in the sense that Thecla is enamored of something other than her role as a virgin bride and potential upholder of her city's values. Theocleia, all too aware of the threat Thecla poses to the social order (and perhaps Theocleia's own standing within it, like that of Perpetua's father), calls for her daughter's burning as an "unbride" (*anymphon*), one who is "lawless," and who, like the Roman *noxii*, threatens the state and its stability through deviant religious practices.

But just as the martyrs were delivered from their pain because they were prepared to suffer for God, Thecla, led to the pyre, is delivered by divine intervention from being burned: God sends a sweeping hailstorm to put out the blaze (22): "Thus ends the first part of her story, the destruction of a former identity and the emergence of a new one, as the unassailable and powerful virgin slave girl of God," without an earthly master (Streete, 2009: 84). The death of her old identity is reinforced when she meets Paul and his host family at a tomb, where she declares that she has essentially risen from the flames. Paul, however, hesitates to let Thecla become his disciple, because her beauty might be a temptation: he offers the torturous argument that although she would not tempt him, she might herself be tempted to fail at "enduring" and thus to "act like a cowardly man" (Streete, 2005: 270). It seems that Paul here is treating Thecla like a woman who could potentially act like a man but has not yet completed the process and thus is threatening to him because of her dangerous femininity (which is possibly his own male fallibility).

As in the stories of the female martyrs, Thecla's beauty and feminine appearance are emphasized only to prove their ultimate insignificance. Following Paul to Antioch, Thecla is accosted by the Asiarch Alexander, in a parody of the Greek romance theme of "love at first sight." For Alexander, however, it is lust at first sight: he believes the lone Thecla is a loose woman and that Paul is her pimp. When questioned, Paul shamefully repudiates Thecla, saying he does not know her nor is she "his," leaving her to the tender mercies of Alexander: when she refuses his advances, he condemns her to the beasts (27). Clearly, as in Iconium, so also in Antioch, Thecla's "crime" is to refuse to assume the role assigned her as a freeborn female citizen: she will not marry or submit to sexual intercourse; therefore, she is "an affront to the social order" (Streete, 2009: 87) and must be executed as a "sacrilege" (28. 32).

Unlike the situation in Iconium, however, Thecla finds support in the women of Antioch, especially the noble Tryphaena, who protects Thecla and keeps her "pure" – not subject to rape or violation in prison – until her trial in the arena. Tryphaena becomes a replacement mother to Thecla, her motherhood all the more emphasized because she is grieving for her own dead daughter, Falconilla. In a possible reminiscence or echo of the visions of Perpetua about her dead brother Dinocrates, Falconilla appears to her mother in a vision and asks her to request that Thecla pray for her, that she might be "translated to the place of the just" (28). Tryphaena nevertheless cannot prevent Thecla from appearing in the arena: she must endure her *agon*, in the manner of other martyrs. The beasts she faces, however, a lioness and a she-bear (we may be meant to think of Perpetua and Felicitas being matched with a wild heifer, "suitable to their sex") can kill her: the lioness, in fact, defends her, until she herself is killed. Thecla's survival does not mean she is released: although even the governor of Antioch weeps for the coming destruction of her beauty, he condemns her again to beasts, this time to ravening seals. Undaunted, Thecla treats this occasion as an opportunity to seize for herself the baptism Paul has denied her: she leaps into the water with the seals, claiming, "I am baptized [or I baptize myself] in the name of Jesus Christ on the last day!" (34). Thecla's action is obviously approved by God, because he causes a lightning bolt to kill the seals (fortunately, Thecla escapes being electrocuted), and a cloud to cover up her naked-ness, her virgin's modesty a concern of the narrator, just as Perpetua's modesty in mending her torn dress and fixing her disheveled hair is emphasized by the narrator of her martyrdom.

The "seal" of baptism, the mark of belonging to Christ together with her resolute chastity for Christ protect Thecla in her last two trials of combat with the beasts. Again, God rescues her from assault by causing the ropes that bind her to be burnt through: "Lust's last assault is finished" (Streete, 2009: 88), and the governor "marvels" at the force field that surrounds Thecla. This final miracle, in a Greek romance, would be the opportunity for the happy ending. But since this is an anti-romance, the reunion of Paul and Thecla is not one of two sundered lovers, but as two apostolic equals. Thecla travels to Myra, wearing a man's clothes, together with her own male and female followers, and finds Paul. Their reunion is rather disappointing: Paul is "astounded" to see her and still imagines that "some other temptation was with her" (40). Thecla, however, is emboldened by the baptism that she has given herself. Perhaps with relief, Paul sends her back to Iconium, with the words, "Go, and preach the word of God" (41). Commissioned by the apostle Paul, Thecla herself becomes an apostle, "a traveling evangelist," essentially becoming Paul rather than being united with him, a celibate itinerant rather than a married householder (McLarty, 2018: 229).

3.1 Persecution for Chastity

Thecla's story is one on a spectrum of narratives of holy women persecuted and even martyred for their choice, not simply of chastity in marriage but for the more extreme form of chastity: celibacy before, within, and outside of marriage. In their stories, Christian rhetoric was once again using Roman moral values – chastity and self-control – and shifting their emphasis away from their locus in familial duty and civic virtue (Cooper, 1996: 17). Syrian Christianity in particular, with its "ascetic" understanding of religious faith (Brock and Harvey, 1987: 7) contains several martyrologies in which women who had made their choice for celibacy and the virgin life, by becoming "daughters of the covenant," were given the choice of marriage, exposure in a brothel, or martyrdom. Martha, daughter of Posi, is urged to save her life by marrying, having children, and renouncing this "disgusting" covenant of celibacy. She refuses because she is "betrothed to Christ," for which she is "slaughtered like a lamb" (*Martyrdom of Martha, Daughter of Posi, who was a Daughter of the Covenant*, 240; Brock and Harvey, 1987). In his treatise *On Virgins*, Bishop Ambrose of Milan praises the example of Thecla as one that should teach virgins "how to be offered [martyred]," because of her "refusal of nuptial intercourse," which changed even the disposition of the wild beasts intended for her slaughter, ceasing because of their reverence for virginity (*On Virgins*, 2.3.19). Ambrose also holds up the example of another legendary virgin, Agnes, who as a girl of twelve refused marriage as a mark of conversion during the persecution of Diocletian, urging the executioner not to delay, but to take her tempting body out of this world: "One victim, but a twofold martyrdom: Agnes preserved her virginity and gained a martyr's crown" (*On Virgins*, 1.2.8–9). Jerome also commends Agnes, who "by her martyrdom hallowed the very name of virginity" (Jerome, *Letter* 130.5). Christian women who were martyred because of their choice of celibacy removed themselves from the world and from the church: they could be admired and imitated, but they did not provide models for authority in the church, as did Thecla.

3.2 "My Sister, My Spouse": Ascetic Women as Brides of Christ

Agnes' refusal of marriage is prompted by her belief that her true spouse is Christ: to have an earthly bridegroom is therefore to commit adultery, as in the story of Martha, daughter of Posi. Similarly, Mary, niece of Abraham, believes that in losing her virginity she has sinned against her "heavenly bridegroom," Christ (*Mary, Niece of Abraham of Qidun*, 18; Brock and Harvey, 1987). In the *Acts of Paul and Thecla*, when Thecla is condemned to be burned as an "unbride" by the Iconians, led by her mother and the civic authorities, she believes that she is actually already married to a heavenly bridegroom and cannot commit adultery against him. Marriage to Christ and fidelity to him are often the Christian justification for female celibacy, playing on the Roman regard for wifely chastity. As Elizabeth Clark (2008: 2) notes, "Although a young virgin's rejection of earthly nuptials might shock the aristocratic society of the late Roman Empire, she [i.e., Thecla] could nevertheless be imaged as *someone's* wife."

In the *Symposium* of Methodius, which substitutes female Christian celibacy for Greek homoeroticism, Thecla leads other virgins in an *epithalamium*, a song traditionally sung at a wedding, at the entrance to the bridal chamber, but here, for the "marriage" of the "celibate bridegroom," Christ, to the virginal church, represented by the twelve virginal "apostles" of the symposium. In the *Apocryphal Acts of Thomas*, the apostle Thomas converts a young bride and groom to practice continent marriage at the very entrance to their bridal chamber, by singing an *epithalamium* in praise of celibacy.

When advising young women like Paula's daughter Eustochium against earthly marriage, the ascetic church father Jerome is quite eloquent about its drawbacks: "pregnancy, the crying of infants, the torture caused by a rival, the cares of household management" (Jerome, *Letter* 27.2). These belong to the unappetizing legacy – unappetizing from a male perspective – of worldly intercourse. Marriage to Christ, on the other hand, confers on a virgin royal status. In his allegorical interpretation of Psalm 45:13, a favorite of clerical advocates for virginity, the virgin is not only the "king's daughter," who is "all glorious within" her chamber, symbolic of her virginity, but is also to be the wife of the heavenly king. Consequently, Jerome addresses Eustochium, "the Lord's bride," as "lady" (*domina*). He also quotes constantly (more than twenty times) from the Song of Songs, another allegorical favorite of the church fathers, as he commends the true spiritual eroticism of this heavenly marriage that is all honeymoon and dalliance and no drawback:

> Ever let the privacy of your chamber guard you; ever let
> your Bridegroom sport with you within. Do you pray?
> You speak to the Bridegroom. Do you read? He speaks to
> you. When sleep overtakes you He will come behind and
> put His hand through the hole of the door, and your heart
> shall be moved for Him; and you will awake and rise up
> and say: I am sick of love. Then He will reply: A garden
> enclosed is my sister, my spouse; a spring shut up,
> a fountain sealed. (Letter 27.25)

In a similar letter to the young virgin Demetrias, who has had the courage to "come out" to her parents as a celibate and to refuse an aristocratic marriage in preference to virginity, Jerome cites a ceremony in which a virgin is "consecrated" ritually by the bishop as a bride to Christ, again citing verses from Psalm 45, in which the virgin is actually called the "daughter of the king" and Christ is the king (*Letter* 130.7; Clark, 2008: 11). As has been previously observed, Jerome was not alone among the church fathers in using the highly erotic language of the Song of Songs to elevate and celebrate the symbolic marriage of Christ "quite polygamously – to virgins, widows, to men, to the Church, and indeed, to all Christian believers" (Clark, 2008, 11). Clark cites Alexander of Alexandria, John Chrysostom, Eusebius of Emesa, Cyprian, Aphrahat, Ephrem Syrus, Athanasius, Ambrose, Basil of Ancyra, and Methodius as evidence that nearly every church father who wrote treatises on virginity at one time or another envisioned Christian virgins to be married to Christ and to have spiritual intercourse with him, thus being incapable of earthly marriage and its "contamination" (Clark, 2008: 11–15). Moreover, marriage to Christ ensured that virgins did not act under their own authority, but under obedience to their heavenly husband. Like the church, the wifely body of Christ (Eph 5:25–32), they were subject to Christ through his representatives, the male church leaders.

   To emphasize this union as fully spiritual rather than physically erotic, as often as the church leaders who give advice to celibate women praise the disfiguration of their appearance as female, becoming thin, pale, tottering, with shrinking breasts (Jerome advises Eustochium to bind her breasts tightly, thus disguising her female shape), they also emphasize the "beauty" of their spiritual bodies as brides of Christ. In the early Christian world, for female martyrs as well as for female ascetics, physical beauty, a means of sexual attraction, was perceived as dangerous to spiritual life. It had to be transformed, by removing from the earthly body the social markers of feminine beauty, to emphasize and to develop inner, spiritual beauty, symbolized by the king's daughter who is "glorious" but only within her (virginal) chamber, or the enclosed garden and sealed fountain of the Song of Songs.[13]

3.3 Ideal Celibates: Women in the Apocryphal Acts of the Apostles

The various versions of Thecla's story show her facing martyrdom, but miraculously escaping it by the intervention of God, the miracles ratifying her difficult choice of celibacy. The power of her decision, despite its ability to disrupt and destroy her household, is iterated in other apocryphal Acts, in which the choice of the ascetic life is a similarly empowering one for women, both those who are married and those whose destiny would be marriage, if not for their choice. In this sense, the apocryphal Acts function as propaganda for a choice that leads to autonomy and authority, even as it challenges and undermines existing civic values and the role of women in their respective societies (Burrus, 1987: 2; Streete, 1986: 154). If martyrdom became a route to attain the resurrection body and the immediate life eternal through death, asceticism, as expressed largely through virgin celibacy, was the way to live the "life of the angels" while in the mortal body here on earth, as the third-century writer Methodius asserts in his *Symposium*, which features Thecla as the main speaker. Praising virginity at the banquet of virgins, Thecla declares that *partheneia*, virginity, is *partheia*, equality to God (Methodius, *Symposium* 8.1).

As in many of the martyrologies, most of the women depicted in these apocryphal tales belong to the pagan[14] elites of the empire: wealthy,

---

[13] On notions of beauty, physical and spiritual, in the ancient Roman and early Christian world, see Moss, 2019: 90–113.

[14] There is no good substitute for the term "pagan," which is usually used for non-Christian Romans, not including Jews.

aristocratic women, who were expected to shore up the state by the most basic form of a citizen's duty, the propagation of children, and the raising of those children to shoulder their civic duties in return. The resistance to these ideals was written on the bodies of the women who made the choice for renunciation as surely as it was on the bodies of the martyrs. As in the martyr stories, the ascetic woman's power helps to defeat the demonic powers of this world, represented by non-Christian Roman society, and to win a victory for God against them. Again, as in the martyr stories, these women are described as "noble athletes" and "champions" as they contend for the cause of God. The apocryphal Acts depict the conversion of women by male apostles to a Christianity that is understood as celibate and which, as in the story of Thecla, is actively contested by their high-status families and households. The correctness and power of their choice is nonetheless proven, as in the case of Thecla, through the miraculous powers granted by God because of this choice. In several of these texts, the male apostle disappears after converting his female disciple, either being threatened with or actually suffering execution because of his "perversion" of the woman, or else his role is downplayed: in the end, he is simply the catalyst for the woman's conversion (Burrus, 1987: 43). For example, in a version of the *Acts of Andrew*, a young virgin (unnamed), called an "ascetic champion," defeats a demonic power unleashed on her by a magician. Vanquished because of her resistant purity, the demon instead possesses her brother. While the girl is told that the apostle Andrew can heal her brother, he tells her that the demon has already been routed, thanks to the "holy hands" of the virgin sister (*Pap. Copt. Utrecht* 10.6–8; 14.30).[15]

Thecla's story is perhaps the best known of several on a spectrum of women persecuted and facing martyrdom for their choice of celibacy, and those likewise delivered miraculously because of it. In other apocryphal Acts, married women are also converted to abstinence. An interesting early

---

[15] Magicians are often combatants in stories of the Christian apostles, claiming to possess power but defeated by the power of Christ as embodied by the apostle, for example, Simon Magus in Acts 8:18–24. Several tales of the Syrian holy women depict their persecution by "Magi," or "Magians," their Zoroastrian opponents, who are portrayed as resentful sorcerers.

instance of an elite Christian convert, a female martyr *manquée* and potential ascetic, occurs in Justin Martyr's *Second Apology*, even though here the focus is not so much on the unnamed matron as upon her Christian teacher and pagan husband (Buck, 2002: 542). According to Justin (2 Apol 2:1–20), a Roman matron (unnamed) described as "self-controlled," who tried to persuade her licentious and intemperate husband to join her in a sober Christian life, could not get him to reform. When she threatened divorce, he was so outraged that he accused her to the emperor of being a Christian. When she appealed to the emperor to get her affairs in order before her trial, assuming because of her status that she had such affairs – he granted her request. The husband then accused her Christian teacher Ptolemaeus, who was arrested, tried, tortured, and executed along with two other Christians. The matron subsequently vanishes from the story. She does not undergo martyrdom, nor is it clear that she renounces anything except the husband, a case of the failure of the advice Paul gave to couples in mixed marriages in 1 Cor 7:11–12, on remaining together in the hope of conversion. This may be yet another case of a Christian female believer being better at a Roman virtue (self-control) than her pagan spouse. The matron's resistance to and rejection of her husband because of sexual intemperance is a pattern followed by subsequent matrons in the Apocryphal Acts of the Apostles.

The third-century *Acts of Thomas* takes the theme of marital self-control in an encratite direction. In it, the apostle persuades the married noblewoman Mygdonia, wife of Charisius, to abhor even marital intercourse so much that she flees naked from her husband when he will not accept a celibate marriage with her, going Justin's matron one better. When even Thomas tries to persuade her to return, Mygdonia remains steadfast, so far as going to prison with the apostle and her faithful nurse, Marcia, her own first convert. From prison, she converts another noble wife, Tertia. When released miraculously from prison, this "celibate fellowship" is joined by Mnesara, the wife of the king's son," who is "healed of a strange disease" as soon as she gets her husband to join her in a celibate marriage. Thomas recognizes Mygdonia's leadership of this female celibate group by giving her the authority to baptize her "sisters" with "the victorious power of Jesus" (*Acts of Thomas* 157–8; Streete, 1986: 156).

In the fourth-century *Acts of John*, the celibate apostle converts the noble Drusiana, and when she consequently refuses to have intercourse with her husband, Andronicus, he shuts her up in a tomb as punishment (perhaps in recognition that she is symbolically "dead" to him, as Thecla was to her household). Drusiana does die, slain because of Andronicus' unrestrained desire to possess her. Another noble, Callimachus, who also lusts after her, attempts to violate her dead body. Drusiana is miraculously raised from the dead by John, while Callimachus and the venal steward Fortunatus, who has let him into her tomb, are both bitten by a poisonous snake (a reference to the original tempter?) and die. John also raises Callimachus, but Drusiana, having pity on Fortunatus, raises him herself. The ungrateful and unregenerate steward flees these "dreadful people" (*Acts of John*, 80–3; Streete, 1986: 161, n.55).

In these stories, which represent legendary embroidery on the tales of the apostles in the canonical book of Acts, those women who reject the earthly social and sexual roles that are expected of them find their choice ratified by God through miracles that both rescue them and give them power equal to that of the male apostles. Nevertheless, it must not be forgotten that these are idealized, fictional women, women being written about by men as perhaps impossible role models. Just as with Perpetua, Felicitas, and other women martyrs, they are more to be admired than imitated (Augustine, *Sermon* 280.1.1), and any claims to authority within the church that invoke the example of these women are marginalized by church fathers like Tertullian, who, while praising women martyrs, vilifies as "impudent" any woman who claims the authority of Thecla to teach and baptize (*On Baptism*, 17).

3.4 "Real" Renouncers: The Desert Mothers, Jerome's Circle and the Lausiac History

As fictionalized narratives about women, perhaps adapted from legendary material and used in the service of Christian encratite propaganda (D. MacDonald, 1985: 90–1), the Apocryphal Acts also served as a defense of those "committed to the virgin state" who by the end of the 200s faced a new and different threat of persecution: "attempts at sexual violence" and threats of "condemnation to the brothels" (Brown, 1988: 192). In the ancient world, "life-long lay celibacy was rare" for women and even rarer for men (Burkert, 1985: 98). Celibate marriage was unthinkable: it undermined the very foundation of society by its failure to produce children. Even the majority of the Christian clergy, as Peter Brown (1988: 25) notes, were initially as averse to "disrupt[ing] the institution of marriage as they had been to contemplate the abolition of household slavery," with the possible exception of the as-yet-unmarried young. Even among pagan authors, however, there were arguments for the primacy of virginity over marriage. In the second half of the first century, the physician Soranus discusses the question of "Whether Permanent Virginity Is Healthful"; he contends that those virgin priestesses who are "in service to the gods" are less susceptible to disease, while those who are overweight and have difficulty menstruating are so, not because of virginity but because of "idleness and inactivity" (*Gynecology*, I.vii.31). Because bodies of both men and women are "made ill by desire," permanent virginity for men and women both is healthful, even though Soranus admits, perhaps reluctantly, that intercourse is "consistent with the general principle of nature" (I.vii.30–2). Furthermore, it was necessary for those who could not achieve the virgin life to create the progeny that not only would continue civic life and its public virtues but who could also furnish support for those who chose the opposite: withdrawal from civic life altogether.

As Aline Rouselle (1988: 131) points out, "asceticism in general may be explained by the aim of recapturing the heroism of martyrdom," but also by the literal acceptance of Jesus' words in Matthew 19:12, on making oneself a "eunuch for the sake of the Kingdom of Heaven," and Paul's argument for sexual self-restraint to focus on the "affairs of the Lord" in 1 Corinthians 7. Adopting their example, "the first Christian writings on sexuality were addressed [by men] to women: Tertullian's *On the Veiling of Virgins* and Cyprian's *Virgins and Their Apparel*" (Brown, 1988: 202). Asceticism made its appeal not only to men but also especially to women. Peter Brown observes, "By the year 300," a short time before the last empire-wide persecution of the Christians, and about a decade before the Edict of Toleration made Christianity legal, "Christian asceticism, invariably associated with some form or other of perpetual sexual renunciation, was a well-established feature of most regions of the Christian world" (Brown, 1988:

202). Young men and women dedicated to the celibate life were found "piled up, like pack-ice," around Christian communities (Brown, 1988: 192), while men and women alike sought solitude in the deserts of Egypt, Palestine, and Syria to pursue the life of withdrawal not only from sexual but also from social intercourse. Withdrawal into the desert to pursue the life of an anchorite (literally, "withdrawer") symbolized "total rejection of and alienation from society" (A. Elliott, 1988: 92). But as the *Life of Anthony*, the laudatory biography of one of the most celebrated of anchorites, shows, withdrawal was simply an invitation for visits from lay society and from other monastics, all hoping for contact with a holy power. As Brown notes of the *Life of Pachomius*, the renouncer who may be regarded as one of the founders of Egyptian monasticism, people prayed, "Send me a man, that I may seek salvation from him" (Brown, 1982: 149). In Pseudo-Basil's *Life and Miracles of St. Thecla*, the saint shuns Seleucia and its "idolatry," living in a cave outside the city, but she is nonetheless constantly consulted, particularly by women, for advice (even about marriage), for healing, and for miracles (Streete, 2009: 98).

As the collected sayings of the desert fathers and mothers demonstrate, however, male and female anchorites and hermits fought their demons differently. Male ascetics like Jerome were in constant despair about their inability to combat sexual desire and vanquish it once and for all, even by withdrawing into the desert. After abandoning the temptations of Rome, and despite all attempts to mortify his flesh, he expresses his frustration: "My face was pale and my frame chilled with fasting, yet my mind was burning with desire, and the fires of lust kept bubbling up before me when my flesh was as good as dead" (*Letter* 22.7). On the opposite side, the desert mother Amma Sarah "waged war against the demon of fornication for thirteen years," simply by praying for strength; in the end, her ascetic manner of life enabled her to conquer him through the power of Christ (Swan, 2001: 37–8). She even proved herself superior to male ascetics. As related in the *Sayings of Amma Sarah*, two male "great anchorites" visited her, solely "to humiliate this old woman," urging her not to be vain because they condescended to visit her. She says merely, "According to my nature, I am a woman, but not according to my thoughts" (Swan, 2001: 39). Amma Syncletica describes her battle against the demons of worldly desire in the same way that martyrs described their contests: "Those who are great athletes must contend against stronger enemies" (Swan, 2001: 54). Pseudo-Athanasius, her biographer, compares her *agon* to that of the "blessed Thecla," as she imitates her contests "through her virtue and sweaty sufferings" (Pseudo-Athanasius, *Life*, 8). Amma Theodora endorses the distinctly Christian virtue of humility in dealing with demons: not fasting, vigils, or withdrawal, the common practices of the desert ascetics, could overcome them. They tell her, "Nothing can overcome us, but only humility" (*Life*, 67), humility being not only one of the chief Christian virtues, but perhaps one special to women, as Amma Sarah's story also shows. In the *Life* of the Syrian desert mother Susan, the narrator says that "weak, feeble, frail women" are "mightily given courage [against evil spirits] and they mock them as a powerful man mocks a band of children or infants preparing to come to fight against him." Because she recognizes the frailty of the men who come seeking to live alongside her female celibate community, she makes a concession to their inability to withstand temptation, secluding the sisters from the men. Susan faces demons "in the form of men," but "she mocked them, as a mighty man would despise sickly men threatening him" (*Life of Susan*, Brock and Harvey, 1987: 138–9).

These legendary female desert ascetics had their counterparts in the women of noble status who chose the ascetic life but who continued their social role as patronesses. As Gillian Cloke (1995: 6) observes, the fathers of the "patristic" age of Christianity (350–450) – "Augustine, John Chrysostom, Gregory of Nazianzus, Gregory of Nyssa, Palladius, Rufinus, and most conspicuous of all, Jerome" – were "surrounded and supported by women," women who were often of a rank socially higher than that of these clergymen, and who acted as their benefactors, perhaps provoking them by their very status to write material that attempted to level these women socially, and to confine them to primarily although not exclusively female social roles. Macrina, the sister of Basil of Caesarea and Gregory of Nyssa, the latter of whom wrote her laudatory biography, was highly influential in the careers of her brothers, including that of her younger brother Peter, to whom she was 'father, teacher, paedagogue, mother, and counsellor" (Gregory of Nyssa, *Life of Macrina*, 12.13–14). The wealthy Olympias of Constantinople, founder of a large monastic institution for widows and virgins, was a staunch supporter of the church in that city and also of John Chrysostom, even in the controversies that led to his exile. Palladius, also a follower of Chrysostom, and later bishop of Helenopolis, spent a number of years with the desert anchorites in Egypt and Palestine; in his *Lausiac History* (419–420), dedicated to Emperor Theodosius II's imperial chamberlain Lausus, he writes: "It is necessary also to mention in my book certain women with manly qualities, to whom God appointed labours equal to those of men, lest any should pretend that women are too feeble to practice virtue" (Palladius, *Lausiac History*, 41.4–5). Among these aristocratic *gynaikes andreiai* ("manly women") are Veneria, "wife of Vallovicus the count"; Theodora, "wife of the tribune"; Hosia and Adolia; Basanilla, "wife of Candidianus the general"; Photina, "venerable in the extreme, daughter of Theoctistes, the priest near Laodicea"; Chrysostom's own aunt, the deaconess Sabaniana; Avita, her husband Apronianus, and their daughter Eunomia, "all so desirous to please God that they were publicly converted to a life of virtue and continence"; and on this account were "freed from all sin": the virgin Silvania, "sister-in-law of Rufinus, the ex-prefect," who dared to chide a bishop for washing, even with ice water, because he catered too much to the flesh; Olympias, "daughter of Seleucus, the ex-count"; the "blessed" Candida, daughter of a general, renowned for her fasting; and Galasia, "a tribune's daughter" (Palladius, *Lausiac History*, 41:4–5; 55:1–3, 56.1–2; 57.1–3; Castelli, 1986: 63, n.9).

Palladius emphasizes particularly the example of Paula of Rome, "a woman of great distinction in the spiritual life," of whom, according to Palladius, even Jerome was jealous because of her greater spiritual distinction. He includes her daughter Eustochium, whom Jerome advises on the virgin life in his *Letter* 22. Palladius also praises the "thrice-blessed" Melania the Elder, widowed at twenty-two, who decided to lead a life of renunciation as "a female man of God" (*Lausiac History*, 9), spending a good deal of time in Egypt with the desert fathers, about whom she provides Palladius with information and travels with them in their exile to Jerusalem. Her story recalls that of Perpetua, in the sense that she left her minor son with a guardian. Because she had "dressed like a young slave" to serve the fathers, bishops, and priests who were banished by the orthodox prefect of

Alexandria to Palestine, the "consular of Palestine" tried to intimidate her
by throwing her into prison, ignorant of who she was. Like Perpetua,
Melania sees this as an occasion to use her rank: she may be Christ's
slave, but the consular should know her true status: he is suitably apologetic
(46.1–6). She later founds a monastery at Jerusalem, and "as the most
scholarly of late-ancient ascetic women," of whom there were
a considerable number (Clark, 1999: 522), she influenced both of the church
fathers Evagrius Ponticus and Rufinus of Aquileia; for the support of the
latter, she earned the opprobrium of Jerome, who had previously admired
her.

   The story of Melania's granddaughter, the younger Melania, illustrates
the dilemma that young Christian women (and men) of rank and wealth
faced. Was it the higher duty, even if unwillingly undertaken, to raise
offspring for their families and thus to support a Christianized civic life,
a life like that praised by theologians such as Augustine? Although preferring "holy virginity" to marriage, he says that the "sober mind" will prefer
Catholic Christian women who had been married "even more than once" to
non-Christian or heretical virgins (*On Marriage and Concupiscence*, 1.4.5;
Clark, 1983: 56–7). Or was it better to take oneself symbolically out of this
world, renouncing not only possessions but also family, in favor of the
higher "life of the angels," and thus "defrauding even their children?"[16]
The younger Melania's parents, perhaps seeing the elder Melania as too
attractive an example, although Albina, the daughter of the elder and the
mother of the younger Melania, herself later chose the ascetic life, "made
her marry a man of the highest rank in Rome." But the granddaughter,
inspired by tales of her intrepid grandmother, became "unable to perform
her marriage duty," especially after having two sons, both of whom died,
and begged her husband, Pinianus, to "practice asceticism . . . according to
the fashion of chastity," with her, or to "take all my belongings and set my
body free." Pinianus finally agreed to the former, and they both "renounced
the world." Melania is said by Palladius to have further renounced her status

---

[16] Palladius (*Lausiac History*, 66.1–7) admires Verus and Bosporia, who spend all
      their income on the poor and in support of orthodox causes, thus leaving nothing
      for their heirs.

by working along with her slave women, "whom she made her fellow ascetics," and in her monastic group included both slave and free, eunuchs and virgins (*Lausiac History*, 61.1–7).

Needless to say, many if not most of these aristocratic women's choices, however independently made they might seem, were influenced by or modeled after male church leaders like John Chrysostom and Jerome, just as the women of the apocryphal Acts had become "spiritually enamored" of the "charismatic itinerant [male] apostles" (Clark, 1983: 77). As Castelli (1986: 63–4) remarks, "Treatises and homilies on virginity and renunciation had their origins in the third century in Africa and seem to have become a favorite of writers in the fourth century and afterwards." At least a dozen of the church fathers, from Tertullian to Methodius, wrote at least one and several wrote more than one treatises on (female) virginity (Castelli,1986: 63, n.9). Augustine's teacher, Ambrose of Milan, held up the rather impossible ideal of the Virgin Mary, whose life of modesty, fasting, prayer, and vigils he improbably describes, pairing her with the legendary ideal of Thecla: "Let, then, holy Mary instruct you in the discipline of life, and Thecla teach you how to be offered [i.e., die as a martyr]" (*On Virgins*, 2.1.7). Ambrose combines the ideals of virginity and martyrdom in citing the example of Agnes, who refused the marriage that would save her during the Diocletian persecution because of her "Spouse," Christ. Like other women idealized by the fathers, the beautiful young Agnes despises the beauty that attracts men to her: "If eyes that I do not want can desire this body, then let it perish" (1.2.8–9). These stories raise important questions. Did virgin and celibate Christian women follow the direction of male Christian leaders to gain the freedom of and from men by rejecting the social roles their female bodies assigned to them? Or did these male Christian leaders, afraid of the temptation of what they perceived as the "toxic femininity" of the female flesh, seek to transform their women adherents into men, or at least to erase them effectively as female sexual beings? Was it then more acceptable to translate Scripture and debate theology with a "brother" rather than a "sister," or even a superior in rank?

Jerome and his circle, even more than John Chrysostom and his supporters, provide a case in point. Jerome's entourage of aristocratic Roman patronesses, like Lea and Marcella, as well as Paula and her children Blesilla and Eustochium, chose, nearly to a woman, to renounce their privilege in favor of the ascetic life that always entailed celibacy, not simply chastity or sexual continence. But did they do so of their own volition or because of Jerome's urging? Jerome, like other church fathers, prescribed the more stringently restrictive behavior for young unmarried women that he dared not give the wealthy widows or celibate couples on whose support, as a social unequal, he depended. The virgins, however, might be held up as examples. Perhaps to avoid charges of heresy for proscribing Christian marriage, he writes, "I praise wedlock, I praise marriage, but it is because they give me virgins" (*Letter* 22.20). In his often-cited *Letter* 22 to Eustochium, as previously seen, Jerome urges Paula's daughter Eustochium against marriage (*Letter* 22. 26). Paula's other daughter, Blesilla, widowed at twenty, was converted to a life of "fierce asceticism," with a particular emphasis on fasting, through Jerome's influence (T. Shaw, 1998: 106–7). Jerome praises Blesilla's extreme self-abasement that made her physically weak and unattractive, aspects that he praised in a letter to another Christian virgin (*Letter* 39.1). In the same way, the female martyrs' tortures destroyed their bodies and physical beauty to refashion them as spiritual "champions." In his praise of the virgin Eustochium, Jerome commiserates with her because of Blesilla, her sister, who by dying has lost both the "crown of virginity" and the "pleasure of wedlock" (*Letter* 22.15). But in his letter to Blesilla's mother, Paula, he suggests that Blesilla, through the severity of her fasting, which has his approval, and because of the "burning fever" that would eventually cause her death, learned "to renounce her over-great attention to that body which the worms must shortly devour" (*Letter* 38.2). When Blesilla dies, and Jerome is accused of urging her to a course in which she was "killed with fasting" (*Letter* 39.6), he turns ferociously on her grieving mother Paula, citing the example of Melania (on whom he also later turned), who, when her husband was still unburied, lost two of her sons: "Motionless she stood there; then, casting herself at the feet of Christ, she smiled . . . 'Henceforth, Lord,' she said, 'I will serve you more readily, for you have freed me from a great burden'" (39.5).

Encouraging and envisioning the destruction and eventual death of female bodies is not unique to Jerome. As Teresa Shaw observes, Basil of Ancyra urged women, whose sole power over men consisted of their appearance, to erase the attraction of that appearance (*On Virginity*, 3;

T. Shaw, 1998: 236). According to Basil, virgins who, "although clothed in the female body," have "by means of asceticism beaten off the shape engendered from it for the sake of the soul, and have made themselves appear like men through excellence (*aretē*)," an excellence that could also be equated with *andreia* as "manliness," like the Latin *virtus* (Basil, *On Virginity*, 57.60; T. Shaw, 1998: 237). Other accounts of ascetic women task them with making themselves unattractive so that they will not cause men to stray. In an encratite section of the *Apocryphal Acts of John*, the apostle argues with a young man who has killed his father, who tried to keep him away from his neighbor's wife. The apostle raises the father from the dead, but only on the condition that the young man will keep away from "the woman who has become dangerous to you" (48). In the *Life* of Susan, "holy and manly in Christ," a woman who is "stone, and instead of flesh she is iron," the narrator tells us that Susan has not seen a man's face for twenty-five years, not because she would "suffer harm at the sight of a man," but that *he* would be harmed at the sight of *her* (Brock and Harvey, 1987: 133–4, 141). Alexandra, as recounted in Palladius' *Lausiac History* 5.1–3, becomes an anchoress and shuts herself up in a tomb for ten years. When the elder Melania asks her why, she replies, "A man was distressed in mind because of me and, lest I should seem to afflict or disparage him, I chose to take myself alive into a tomb rather than cause a soul made in the image of God to suffer." To avoid the sin of *accidia* (sloth), she prays and spins flax (a typical female occupation) daily. She fills the rest of the time with meditation "on the holy patriarchs and prophets and apostles and martyrs." The matriarchs are not mentioned, but one hopes some of the martyrs she meditates on are female. These and similar texts are composed by men who urge women to become men, or at least to cease being visibly women, thus removing the threat of their dangerous sexuality. For whatever reason, the women oblige, but ironically they appear to be the stronger and not the weaker sex, because of their vigilant and strenuous self-control.

3.5 Repentant Harlots and Cross-Dressing Sisters

A number of tales from this period of late ancient Christianity feature women who have led a life of sexual promiscuity: the so-called harlot saints, who retreat from society, dress as men, and live as male monastics or anchorites. Other women, like Thecla, adopt male attire, perhaps as a protection against attack by lustful men because of their female appearance and solitariness, or for the greater freedom that dressing as a male afforded. Stephen J. Davis (2000: 15–17) mentions the stories of Susannah (*Life of Susannah*) and Eugenia (*Life of Eugenia*), in which the heroines cut their hair and dress in men's clothing, the first to escape a mandated marriage, the second after reading the *Acts of Paul and Thecla*, both imitating Thecla in their quest for the "ascetic vocation." Male dress also signified the transition from a perceived female preoccupation with appearance (an idea largely promoted by male authors) to the public persona adopted by males, especially male monastics, who were markedly careless of their appearance as a means of rejecting the vanity, a mark of worldliness, that was supposed to beset women.

One of the most prominent of the first type of story – the harlot saint – is that of Mary Magdalene, a Magdalene far different from the one in the gospels or the Gnostic writings, where she appears as a follower, benefactor, and teacher (e.g., Lk 8:1–3; Gospel of Mary). In the sixth century, Pope Gregory the Great conflated her with the "woman of the city" in Lk 7:39, who was a "sinner." She may have been combined with other repentant "sinners" as well, including Mary of Egypt, who, according to her *Life*, lives promiscuously in Alexandria but wishes to travel to Jerusalem for the Exaltation of the Cross. Having no capital, she prostitutes herself to gain money for the passage. When she reaches the Holy Sepulcher, she is prevented by a kind of holy force field from entering, but she prays to the "ever immaculate Virgin, who always kept [her] body and soul chaste and clean from all sin" to intercede for her and is able to enter, once she vows "never again [to] defile my flesh by immersing it in horrifying lusts." The Virgin Mary tells her to cross the Jordan River, and the former prostitute lives in the desert for forty-seven years. In an instructive dialogue with the monk Zosima, who has come to visit this phenomenon, Mary reveals how often and how strenuously she fasts, in words that recall those of Jerome about his struggles in the desert but also echo Amma Sarah's about her defeat of the demon of fornication with the help of Christ: "Believe me, father, I struggled for seventeen years with the wild beasts of huge and irrational desires" before prayer to the Virgin enables her to withstand them. She asks Zosima to come again in a year, and to bring her the sacrament, but when he does so, he sees her lying dead, with a written request to bury "Mary the sinner." With the help of a friendly lion, à la Thecla, he is able to dig her grave (Ward, 1987: 56–66).

Another Mary, the niece of Abraham of Qidun, is the heroine of the fourth-century Syriac *Life of Abraham* (17–29; Brock and Harvey, 1987: 24–37). Mary is not mentioned as wearing male garb specifically, but she nevertheless dresses in ascetic garments like those of her uncle, and as a repentant harlot later wears sackcloth. In this narrative, Abraham trains his young niece "to attain to the perfection of his virtues." Mary, however, is seduced (or possibly raped) by a man purporting to be a monk and believes that she has lost all hope of salvation, with the loss of the virginity she was keeping for her "heavenly bridegroom," Christ. She establishes herself as a prostitute in a "low tavern," where she is found by her uncle Abraham, who dresses like a soldier, not only to blend in but also to do battle with the Adversary, Satan. Pretending to be a patron, he asks for the "quite exceptionally beautiful" Mary, raising the question of whether beauty could have led to her downfall, but as she embraces the supposed soldier, she smells "the smell of asceticism" and, reminded of her earlier life, runs away in a panic. To "save one soul," however, Abraham commits the worldly sins of eating meat and sitting on the bed with a woman, but he later reveals his identity to Mary and convinces her that she can be forgiven if he intercedes for her. Mary goes beyond his forgiveness to repentance, leaving behind her fine clothes and ill-gotten gains, dresses in "sackcloth and humility," and engages in the repentant practices of weeping and nightly vigils. When Abraham dies, Mary keeps weeping, but at the time of her own death, her face is radiant, showing the power of her redemption.

The tale of Pelagia of Antioch, referred to in John Chrysostom's *Homily on Matthew* 67.3 simply as "that harlot that went beyond all in lasciviousness," is perhaps "a reworking of a pagan romance" (Brock and Harvey, 1987: 40, n.4). The romantic theme is combined with "the theme of a woman who disguises herself as a monk [who] was to become something of a historical [Christian] *topos*" (41). On his initial encounter with Pelagia, she appalls the good bishop Nonnos as he is preaching, when she comes by with her entourage, gorgeously adorned with pearls, silk, and precious stones: her perfume alone is alluring (Jacob, *Life of Pelagia*, 4–6). Despite her beauty and this shameless display, Pelagia is dressed "almost like a man," because she is not "covered" like a woman, or because prostitutes, as public persons, would dress like men (6). Bishop Nonnos is less appalled by her "shamelessness" than he is "astonished at her beauty" and is saddened that she is a "snare and a stumbling block" to others (7–8). As Nonnos preaches, albeit without rhetorical skill, because he has had no secular education (an indication of his sincerity and divine inspiration), Pelagia comes into the church and is moved by the homily that already has driven the congregation to tears: she herself groans and sobs "loudly." At the shrine of the "glorious martyr Julian," Pelagia prostrates herself and confesses that she is "Satan's evil snare," begging for an immediate baptism, to make her a "bride of Christ" (18–26). With the aid of Romana, the head deaconess of the church, she is baptized, recalling baptisms of women by women in the apocryphal Acts (28–9). Romana thus becomes Pelagia's spiritual mother. When Satan inevitably appears, as he always does at baptisms, in a last attempt to prevent Pelagia's "sealing" by Christ, she is able to rebuke him: she and Romana make the sign of the cross, and he is gone (31–3). Adopting an ascetic lifestyle, Pelagia, "dressed as a man" disappears into the desert.

Later, the deacon Jacob, the purported author of her *Life*, is told to seek out "a certain monk Pelagius, a eunuch," who is "perfect in his service," living on the Mount of Olives in Jerusalem (43). When Jacob visits her/him, he finds that

> she [as Pelagia] had lost those good looks I used to know, her astounding beauty had all faded away, her laughing and bright face that I had known had become ugly, her pretty eyes had become hollow and cavernous as the result of much fasting and the keeping of vigils. The joints of her holy bones, all fleshless, were visible beneath her skin through emaciation brought on by ascetic practices. Indeed the whole complexion of her body was coarse and dark like sackcloth. (45)

Toxic, seductive femininity has been routed into holy ugliness through asceticism. Jacob, moreover, does not notice anything about "her" that would indicate she is a woman, noting only that she was a "male eunuch who was a renowned monk, a perfect and righteous disciple of Christ." Pelagia/Pelagius has become a "man of God" and erased any signs of her being female. Only when s/he dies and a "great crowd" of clergy and laity has gathered to anoint the saint's body, do they find she is a woman. They then praise God for the "hidden saints," and "not just men, but women as well!" (49). Hiding herself as a woman, essentially becoming a man, Pelagia has thereby become a saint.

Another repentant harlot, Thaïs, is also a courtesan from Alexandria, "wealthy and beautiful," a standard description of the women in these tales. When one of the most famous of the desert fathers, Paphnutius, visits her in a secular guise, he warns her about the coming judgment, and she immediately repents, "burned all of her goods," and departs for the desert, following Paphnutius' example. There she immures herself in a cell attached to a convent, in the classic female anchoritic tradition. When Paphnutius visits her later, offering her forgiveness for her sins, she insists on staying where she is and dies shortly afterward (*Life of Thaïs*, Ward, 1987: 76–7).

In a cycle of narratives from the late sixth century, the noble Anastasia, in the tradition of holy fools, at first appears to be a "mad girl" and is mistreated by her fellow nuns; however, when she demonstrates holy power, she leaves the convent, dressed in male attire, perhaps confirming that this power has made her a man. Later, the two monks who had initially visited the convent and discovered the apparently mad but holy Anastasia and chastised the nuns for their treatment of her are sent by their superior to visit "an old man, a eunuch." The dying eunuch prays that they will not unclothe him for his burial, but when one of them seeks to put another garment on top of what "he" is wearing, he notices "women's breasts, shriveled up like leaves." One of the disciples then informs his master that the "eunuch" was a woman, and the master tells him the following story. She was a patrician lady of the highest rank under the emperor Justinian and was also a deaconess of the church. The emperor wanted to introduce her to his court, not only because of her beauty but also because of her great virtue. His jealous wife, the empress Theodora, sent her into exile.

Anastasia fled the court to Alexandria, where the emperor pursued her after Theodora's death. Again she fled – this time to Skete in Egypt, renowned home of monastics, where she received a man's clothes and lived as a man for twenty-eight years. The narrator said the lesson of this story was as follows: "See, my son, how many people have been brought up at court, yet have performed battle against the adversary, battering their bodies, and living like angels on earth" (*Life of Anastasia*, 5–9; Brock and Harvey, 1987: 145–8). Like Anthony, Anastasia flees further and further from society, which continues to praise her as "she" becomes "he" and is victorious over the power of the female flesh that is a snare to men.

Another cross-dressing saint, Hilaria, supposedly the daughter of the Byzantine emperor Zeno, fled her privileged life "disguised as a [male] knight" and eventually joined one of the monasteries at Sketis [Skete] in Egypt, where she become renowned for her feats of "ascetic endurance and self-renunciation" (Davis, 2000: 20) and became ordained as a monk under the name of "Hilary," presumed a eunuch. Through her ascetic practice, s/he ceases to be identified physically as a woman: her breasts are "shrunken with ascetic practice," and her menses cease (28, n.70; *Life of Hilaria*, 6.75). When her sister Thaopesta becomes ill, her parents send her to the renowned eunuch, Hilary, at Sketis to be healed by "his" prayer. Thaopesta is healed, but she enjoys an intimacy with the supposed eunuch that makes the emperor suspicious, so that he sends for the eunuch. In the end, Hilary/Hilaria is compelled to confess who s/he is. Although the imperial couple are reluctant to lose their daughter a second time, s/he goes back to Sketis, where five years later s/he dies, no one knowing his/her identity as a woman until after his/her death (*Coptic Orthodox Church Network*, Commemorations for Toba 21). As Davis (2000: 21) notes, Hilaria's *Life* imitates that of Anthony, especially in his anchoritic practice and is "understood to be actualizing a distinctively male piety" (29). Similarly, in the *Life of Matrona*, the heroine "flees her abusive husband, disguises herself as a eunuch called Babylas, and enrolls in a male monastery in Constantinople," where she is "completely transformed into a man" (29). Davis also points out that the friends who have helped Matrona to his/her transformation are named Eugenia and Susannah, thus referring to other stories of "women disguised as men," while s/he eventually ends up at the monastery of the "blessed Hilaria," a reference to another cross-dressing saint (31).

As Davis (2000: 32) suggests, the categories of male and female are "de-stablilized" in these narratives, perhaps expressing Paul's claim in Gal 3:27–8 that "in Christ" binary categories like male and female have been dissolved. In his sermons, Augustine also suggests a similar ambiguity of identity in the martyr narrative of Perpetua and Felicitas: "According to the inner human, [they were] found to be neither male nor female" and thought "women in body," their bravery of mind "took away the sex of their flesh" (*Sermon* 280.1.1). I would suggest, however, that in the case of cross-dressing saints, female identity is decisively rejected, and male identity is claimed and valorized as a marker of a superior way of living. These "female men of God" are performing masculinity. Indeed, as Castelli (1986: 77) observes, "manliness" (*andreia*) is used to describe ascetic women from the time of *the Shepherd of Hermas* in the early second century. The spiritual "life of the angels," as depicted in the narratives of ascetic women who dress and live as men, is one of women deliberately erasing a female identity to become male, much as Jesus says to Peter in the Gospel *of Thomas*, Saying 114, that he will make Mary (Magdalene) male, that she will become "a living male spirit, similar to you. . . . Every woman who makes herself male will enter the Kingdom of Heaven" (*Fifth Gospel*, 32). T. Shaw (1998: 246) notes the physical effects of strenuous ascetic practices, especially fasting, on the bodies of women: "If we consider the protological association of sexuality, death, and the fall with the female, or with gender differentiation and hierarchy, then for a female ascetic to mortify her body to the point of unrecognized femaleness, even to the point of sterility, is truly to return to paradise."

3.6 Dismembering and Disfiguring Female Bodies

Women martyrs become men by having their female bodies disfigured by torture, mutilation, and dismemberment; women ascetics become men by eroding their female bodies through severe practices like fasting to refashion them as far as possible into those of males. If in both cases, the goal is an "imagined return to paradise," then, as Candida Moss (2019: 17) has aptly said, "It is here . . . that our values are most nakedly displayed," often quite literally. Clearly, the premier value to be displayed is that of manliness or

manly courage – but why? What could possibly have motivated these
women to adopt this male value for themselves, if indeed they actually
did so? There is precious little evidence from the women: Perpetua's prison
diary, if it is authentically hers,[17] in which she seems rather to morph into
a man than to achieve manhood, and the sayings of the desert mothers
(collected from an oral tradition). Some of the Apocryphal Acts may have
originated in orally circulated tales of celibate and independent widows
(Burrus, 1987; Davies, 1980; D. MacDonald, 1985), but that is conjectural
(Kraemer, 2011: 150). We also have an exchange of letters between Melania
the Elder and Evagrius Ponticus, preserved in Armenian (Castelli, 1986: 62,
n.4). Otherwise, we have the writings of a large number of male Christian
leaders who either dictated these women's actions or speculated on their
motives and used their examples for *men* to admire and imitate, lest they be
shamed into being less "manly" than these "female men of God." If women,
perceived as weak by nature, could perform extraordinary feats of bodily
endurance in the arena and bodily confidence in the monastic cell, why
should not men, the stronger in body and more spiritual by nature, do the
same? To quote Augustine on the case of Perpetua and Felicitas, these
women were the equals of even the "bravest of men," their male comrades,
"not so much because women should surpass men in the dignity of their
morals, but because even a women's weakness conquered the ancient enemy
[i.e., Satan] by a greater miracle, and manly virtue fought for perpetual
felicity" (*felicitas perpetua*; *Sermon* 282.3; Streete, 2009: 62). Tertullian even
goes so far as to say that Perpetua saw "only martyrs" on her entry into
Paradise that was closed to Eve but opened by the martyr's redemptive
death not only to women but also to men (*On the Soul*, 55.5).

4 Bodies That Save the World

The bodily endurance and sexual continence of these women, martyrs and
ascetics alike, serve as a means of redemption, not only for the women
themselves, redeeming the "sin of Eve," but also for others. As with

---

[17] On the authenticity of Perpetua's diary, see the summary by Hunink (2016:
146–55).

Perpetua and Thecla, martyrs and confessors are depicted as having the ability to free others from the consequences of their sins in the next life and even to perform reconciliation on earth and in heaven. By transforming themselves, effectively ceasing to be women in body, the ascetic women and virgins especially were able to redeem the fallenness of their female sexual nature and to sanctify others as well, following the example of Mary, the "mother of virgins," who, according to Ambrose, "worked the salvation of the world ... the redemption of all" (*Letter* 49.2). While condemning the worship of Mary by the sect known as the Collyridians, and women's ministry in general, Epiphanius declares nevertheless that Mary is the virgin who remedies the "defect" of Eve (*Medicine Box*, 79.2–3, 9; Streete, 1999: 348).[18] The fourth-century Canons of Athanasius even go so far as to say that virginity has a vicarious power of salvation: "In every house of Christians, it is needful that there be a virgin, for the salvation of that whole house is one virgin. And when wrath comes upon the whole city, it shall not come upon the house wherein a virgin is" (98.62–3; Streete, 1999: 348). Augustine does not share that view. In his *City of God*, citing the rape of dedicated virgins during the sack of Rome by the Arian Alaric and the Visigoths (410), he asserts that this disaster may have happened lest they take excessive pride in managing their own chastity (*City of God*, 1.16–19). But he urges the women not to feel such shame and defilement as to kill themselves, following the example of Lucretia, since "purity is a state of mind," not body.

4.1 Bodies and Status

As Joyce Salisbury (1991: 29) notes, and as has been shown previously, "The spiritual power that came with a life of chastity was similar to the power martyrs achieved through their sacrifice. Virginity, too, was seen as a sacrifice, a sacrifice of sexuality and personal fecundity." But to sacrifice or renounce property and status, one must have them to begin with. Slave women and many freed or freeborn women of a low social status could not achieve practical sexual renunciation: an important difference between

---

[18] The idea that the Collyridians are a heresy created by Epiphanius has been challenged by Ally Kateusz (Kateusz, 2013: 75–42, 2019: 19–51).

martyrdom and asceticism. Even the sex worker Pelagia was rich and independent (*Life of Pelagia of Antioch*, 4; John Chrysostom, *Homily on Matthew*, 67.3). The stories of martyred women slaves like Felicitas and Blandina demonstrate that in death for Christ, the "worthless," weak, and even "ugly" bodies of slave women were ennobled. In Eusebius' recounting of the martyrdoms at Lyons and Vienne (*HE* v.1.3–28), the pagan slaves of Christian masters, fearful of the tortures that they saw the latter suffering and fearing justifiably for those they might themselves suffer, accused their masters of incest and cannibalism, the usual charges against Christians in the Roman Empire. On the contrary, the slave Blandina's "mistress in the flesh" fears that Blandina's body will break under torture "because of her bodily weakness," but Blandina is filled with such power that even her torturers grow weary and exhausted. After she is exposed in the arena and subjected to more tortures, Blandina, "tiny, weak, and insignificant," is transformed into Christ, "that mighty and invincible athlete," and even into a "noble [*eugenēs*] mother," a status that she could not have attained in her earthly existence. Thus Blandina demonstrates that what is thought to be "cheap, ugly, and contemptuous" – the body of a slave woman – has become "worthy of glory before God" (*Martyrs of Lyons and Vienne*, *HE* v.1, 17).

In the *Martyrdom of Perpetua and Felicitas*, the slave woman Felicitas is taken to the prison when she is eight months pregnant. We do not know the father of her child: it may have been her master, or another slave. Unlike Perpetua's son, whose father is similarly absent, but who is cared for by her own father's family, of which he may well be the heir, Felicitas' daughter is given up at birth to be raised by another Christian woman, a "sister." Because of her status, Perpetua is able to make demands, even of her captors, initially to keep her baby with her (*Martyrdom*, 3.9), for better treatment of all the Christian prisoners (16.3) and, finally, for her executioners to remember their agreement not to clothe her (or Felicitas) in the garments of a worshiper of pagan deities (18.5). Even after death, Perpetua retains her status: from heaven, she and the deacon Saturus reconcile two quarreling clergy (13.4), she speaking to them in the educated clerical language of Greek (Streete, 2009: 39). There is no extra-death vision for Felicitas, and no public defense, as with Perpetua. Instead, we witness her suffering, the suffering that foreshadows the *agon* in the arena, when she struggles in prison with the pain of a premature childbirth, while a soldier mocks her by saying that she will soon experience much greater agony. She replies that for now, she struggles alone, but in the arena, she will not be herself: "Another will be in me who will suffer for me, as I also will have suffered for him" (15.6). Like Blandina, the lowly Felicitas, in mirroring the suffering of Christ, who "put on the form of a slave" (Phil. 2:7), has "put on" and therefore become Christ, attaining spiritual power.

Stories about the relationship between ascetic women and their servants, before and after their renunciation, are more problematic. The elder Melania may have dressed like a slave; however, as we have seen, she, like Perpetua, could still pull aristocratic rank (*Lausiac History*, 46.1–6). Melania the Younger works with her slave women, whom she has "made" her fellow ascetics, but are they still her slaves? Did they choose, following her example, to become ascetics? Palladius, her admirer, does not tell us. It may be that an ascetic life of working along with their earthly mistress was preferable to being nothing more than exploitable sexual property. But Melania's toiling along with her slave women seems like a Marie Antoinette – like a pose of simplicity when set alongside the Latin *Life of Melania*, according to which she and her husband Pinianus still owned slaves on their vast properties even after their renunciation and were concerned that a slave rebellion on their estate near Rome would spread to other estates in "Spain, Campania, Sicily, Africa, Mauretania, Britain, and other lands" (*Life*, 11; Clark, 1986: 77).

Other stories of ascetic women, particularly those who suffered martyrdom for their choice, imply equality. In the Syrian *Martyrdom of Tarbo, Her Sister, and Her Servant*, Tarbo's (unnamed) servant, like her mistress, is "pure and chaste," a "daughter of the covenant" (*Martyrdom*, 254) and is martyred along with her and her sister, ignominiously left "naked by the roadside" (259; Brock and Harvey, 1987: 73–6). In an anti-Jewish epistle (Simeon of Beth Arsham's *Second Letter*; Brock and Harvey, 1987: 105–15), depicting the burning of a Christian church, the maidservants of Ruhm, a woman "of high standing" and beauty, are offered freeborn husbands if they convert to Judaism. They refuse and are martyred (ix). Another servant, the "disagreeable maid" Mahya, who is "always very masculine," accordingly asserts an unusual freedom of speech (*parrhēsia*) for a woman by going about in public urging Christians to battle "the Jews" as killers of Christ. She is dragged by her feet, tied to an ox and a donkey, respectively, and thus achieves status (and "blessedness") in death as a "martyr of Christ" (xviii–xxii). Martyrdom, it seems, can be a great leveler, of both gender and status.

The Apocryphal Acts of the Apostles is more equivocal on the matter of status and gender. We have already seen that the maidservants in the *Acts of Paul and Thecla* weep for "the loss of a mistress" when Thecla chooses the itinerant life of a celibate (*Acts of Paul and Thecla*, 10). In the *Acts of Peter*, Xanthippe, wife of Albinus, "a friend of the emperor," and thus a woman of high status, is converted to the ascetic life by Peter's preaching. When Albinus complains to the prefect Agrippa that his wife denies him his sexual "due," he discovers that Agrippa, too, has lost his concubines to the celibate life as promoted by the apostle, giving the men a reason to seek Peter's execution (*Acts of Peter*, 34[5]).[19] Here, women of higher as well as lower rank are determined to choose asceticism, to the distress of husbands and masters.

The *Acts of Thomas* portrays a triple conversion in conjunction with the wedding of the Indian king's daughter. At the wedding banquet, a Hebrew flute-girl, a woman of slave status who was usually brought in to entertain guests not only with music but sexual favors, serenades Thomas, whom she especially loves. On being asked by the king to bless the young couple's marriage, Thomas preaches the "incorruptible and true marriage" that avoids "filthy intercourse" and converts the bride and bridegroom to celibacy before consummating their marriage. When the angry king's servants seek Thomas in the inn where he was staying, they find the flute-girl weeping because he has not taken her with him. But on being told the story of the conversion of the "princess bride" and her groom, the flute-girl rejoices, because she, too, has "found repose" in the chaste life. Although how this would have been possible, given her profession, is unclear, it is best to remember that this is a Christian tale in which both royal and slave

---

[19] Concubines, who held an intermediate status between slave and free, might be presumed to have greater choice than the merely enslaved.

women find and are able to choose renunciation as the only acceptable form of Christian life (*Acts of Thomas*, 11–15).

Throughout, the *Acts of Thomas* portrays this equality through Christian asceticism. In the Ninth Act, when Mygdonia, wife of Charisius, a relative of the king, is borne on a palanquin by her slaves to hear the apostle preach, he delivers a kind of mini–Sermon on the Mount, with ascetic behavior added, preaching first to the slaves, the "heavy laden," and urging them to "contend in the stadium of Christ," as noble athletes, by embracing chastity, temperance, and holiness, the latter of which is personified as an "invincible athlete." Mygdonia is herself converted by Andrew to the ascetic life and refuses from then on to sleep with her husband, from whom she flees, naked, to spend the night protected by her faithful nurse Marcia. Mygdonia's status as an ascetic is ambiguous, however, at least initially, as she moves from her former state. In the Tenth Act, as she is about to receive the coveted "seal" of baptism as an ascetic Christian, for which it was appropriate to maintain a kind of fast, she asks Marcia to bring her some minimal nourishment, "having regard for my birth" (120), presumably meaning that she is not used to scanty rations and is used to being waited on. In the end, both the high-ranking Mygdonia and her servant Marcia are baptized as (celibate) Christians. Later, at Thomas' invitation, Mygdonia baptizes two other women of high status: Tertia, the wife of King Misdaeus, and Mnesara, the wife of his son Vazan (157), who has already been living with her husband in celibate marriage. Misdaeus and Charisius are utterly outraged at the work the "magician" has done in bewitching their wives, destroying their households, and frustrating their hopes of offspring. They imprison not only Thomas but also all the women as well. In this case, as in the *Martyrdom of Perpetua and Felicitas*, Christian women of differing ranks are treated equally as enemies of the public order. The apostle Thomas recognizes their equality to him and to one another by addressing them as "Daughters and sisters and fellow-servants . . . ministers of my Jesus" (159). When Thomas is martyred, Misdaeus and Charisius seize their wives and "afflict them," but surprisingly, "When they perceived that Mygdonia and Tertia did not obey them, allowed them to live according to their own desire" (169). We are not told what happened to Marcia:

perhaps, as Mygdonia's "mother and nurse," she remains with her as part of the fledgling Christian ascetic community.

A more disturbing and complex situation prevails in the *Acts of Andrew*. Maximilla, wife of the proconsul Aegeates, is converted to celibate Christianity by the apostle Andrew, following her brother Stratocles, who has been converted when Andrew heals his servant. Subsequently, Maximilla refuses sexual relations with her husband and wants to spend all of her time with Andrew, her celibate beloved. She adopts a scheme whereby, acting as her benefactor, she procures a "comely, exceedingly wanton servant-girl named Euclia" (17) to sleep with Aegeates, who supposes that she is his wife. The scheme improbably succeeds for eight months, until Euclia starts making demands of Maximilla commensurate with her supposed status: her freedom, jewelry, and fine clothing, and she becomes boastful and arrogant before her fellow slaves, who finally expose the plot. Using his power as proconsul, Aegeates tortures Euclia until she confesses. Instead of raging against Maximilla for duping him, he spends his fury on the slave Euclia, cutting out her tongue, "mutilating her," and exposing her in the street until she dies and is eaten by dogs. Wishing to keep the affair secret for fear of humiliation, Aegeates crucifies rather than rewards the slaves who revealed the plot. He still loves his wife, but even when she tells him that she loves another "not of this world," and wishes to have intercourse with "it" [*sic*], he cannot "commit any impropriety against the blessed woman, for her pedigree far outstripped his" (23–4). Despite her Christian conversion, Maximilla retains the privilege of her high status, heartlessly exposing her slave to exploitation, torture, and death. She also has a faithful slave named Iphidamia, who accompanies Maximilla to the prison where Andrew is held, thanks to Aegeates' rage at the "disruption" of his household, especially after Maximilla rubs salt in the wound by rushing to the *praetorium* to tell her husband that she has bidden "farewell to wickedness, the mother of the flesh, and to all things pertaining to the flesh" and so will not sleep with him (46[14]), making Aegeates resolve to martyr Andrew by crucifixion. On Andrew's death, Maximilla lives with "the brethren," a life that is "holy and quiet," to the end refusing Aegeates, who kills himself (64[10]). We are not told what happened to the loyal Iphidamia: like Marcia in the *Acts of Thomas*, she may be presumed to have remained with her mistress, but the stories even of faithful slave women are seemingly unimportant when compared with those of high-status converts to the ascetic life. The autonomy that the choice of a life of renunciation secured for women of a higher status as depicted in the *Lausiac History* and the Acts of the Apostles was seldom possible for slave women, who were used for other, worldlier ends, sometimes by the "blessed" aristocratic female renouncers themselves.

4.2 Autonomy: Alleged or Actual?

One might also question whether or not this autonomy, even for the noble female renouncers, was actual. Several scholars have claimed that the women described in the apocryphal Acts and in Palladius' *Lausiac History* did in fact already have virtual autonomy and authority, not only over their own lives but also those of others, and that renunciation of "the world" ironically gave them some further measure of control over it. The apocryphal stories may have been initially told by communities of celibate women, to give other women a template for similar behavior that led to independence but still remained Christian (Burrus, 1987; Davies, 1980; D. MacDonald, 1985; Streete, 1986). Nevertheless, in the emerging orthodox churches of the second century, as evidenced by the Pastoral Epistles (1 and 2 Timothy and Titus), the behavior of women, married and unmarried (or widowed), was a source of concern. Not only were wives not to have authority over their husbands in the church (if we read the *gynaikes* in 1 Tim 2:12 as "wives" more narrowly and not generically as "women"), widows also were subject to regulation by church leaders. The author of 1 Timothy advises the young pastor on how to identify "true" widows: older women who do not have families to support them and therefore need church support (5:4–5). Younger widows, who may have vowed themselves to celibacy as brides of Christ, nevertheless should not be relied on to keep this promise. Like the young widows in Jerome's letters and the *Lausiac History*, these may have been women of high social status, as they seem to have the leisure to "go from house to house," unanchored by the duties of other women (1 Tim 5:13). But widowhood – or even a vow of celibacy – did not for this Pastoral author provide a reason for autonomous behavior (Streete, 1998).

Without question, a good deal of spiritual authority was accorded to women martyrs; however, even if they had become "male" or embodied Christ, they did so when they were on the border between life and death. They had passed from earth, and their authority as ideals was available to be harnessed in the interests of an increasingly male-led church, and not as a reason to give living women authority in it. One has only to recall Tertullian's fulmination against the "impudence" of Quintilla for claiming the authority to teach and baptize, citing the example of Thecla (*On Baptism*, 17). Similarly, Augustine uses Perpetua and Felicitas as models for *men* (the specific *viri* rather than the generic *homines*, *Sermon* 280.1.1). Clark observes that John Chrysostom, writing about the singular institution of celibate women living with celibate men – the so-called *virgines subintroductae* – insisted that "females through martyrdom (in the past) or ascetic devotion (in his own day) might be fortunate enough to appropriate some of the nobler masculine qualities (courage, for example), but nowhere did Chrysostom indicate that women should be praised for assertiveness or the adoption of the types of behavior permitted to men" (Clark, 1986: 280). So it seems that only the anchoritic desert mothers, many of whom, like Amma Syncletica, had been women of some means and social standing, wealthy women like those depicted in the apocryphal Acts, and the aristocratic, educated members of Jerome's and Chrysostom's circles, achieved some form of autonomy. If, like Paula, Melania, and Olympias, they founded ascetic and monastic institutions, then their social standing, even after their choice of the ascetic life, enabled them to have control over these foundations as benefactors and patronesses. Nevertheless, we see what happened when the elder Melania asserted her theological authority and sided with Rufinus and the Origenists: the Jerome who had so praised her as "the new Thecla" punned caustically on her name: "The blackness of her name testifies to the darkness of her perfidy," or, more scurrilously, "Black by name, black by nature" (Jerome, *Letter* 133; Murphy, 1947: 59; Streete, 2006: 202–3).

5 The Bodies of the Blessed

We have seen a number of narratives – martyrologies and hagiographies – that portray what happens to the bodies of female martyrs and ascetics in this world, while anticipating the next. What becomes of these bodies in the afterlife? With its apocalyptic and eschatological orientation, early Christianity had concentrated on the transformation of this world, with only vague speculations about what the "resurrection life" would be like. As previously shown, in his diatribe in 1 Corinthians 15 on what happens to the body in the resurrection, Paul is most emphatic in responding to the possible mocking question, "But how are the dead raised? With what body do they come?" He differentiates between kinds of bodies: the body of a seed is not the body that becomes grain; there are heavenly bodies and earthly bodies, and so on. His point is that a "physical body" is "sown," like grain, but it is raised a spiritual body. For Paul, it is a "mystery" how this transformation occurs (1 Cor 15:35–55). As everyone, men and women alike, were on earth members of the body of Christ, the church, so they will also become a risen, spiritual body like that of the risen Christ: here, Paul does not mention gender.

In the *Martyrdom of Perpetua and Felicitas*, although Perpetua dreams before her martyrdom about being changed into a male gladiator to face down and conquer the devil in the arena, the author of her martyrology later mentions her, along with Saturus, in heaven, clearly identified as their pre-martyred and gendered selves, their authority perhaps enhanced by their heavenly status. According to Clark, Jerome, in his exposition on the post-Pauline position regarding marriage in Ephesians 5, claims that women or wives, whom he calls "bodies," will in the afterlife become men or "souls" (Jerome, *Against Jovinian*, 1.37; Clark, 2008: 21). Under pressure from critics like Rufinus of Aquileia and his adherents, Jerome later changed his position, stating that resurrected bodies would be differentiated as male and female, together with sex organs that they would not use (Jerome, *Apology against Rufinus*, 1.28–9; Clark, 2008: 22). Jerome is not alone in this latter claim: Moss (2019: 86) observes that in the writings of early Christian authors, "nonfunctional genitals become the paradigm of the Kingdom of God." Through ascetic discipline, this transformation might happen even before the arrival into Paradise. The body itself might become the realm of the spiritual, even while dwelling in the physical world.

Hundreds of years after Paul, Augustine responds to similar pagan Roman questions about the resurrected body in the final book (22) of his

City of God, but his answers are far more imaginatively detailed. As summarized in *Seducing Augustine* (Burrus et al., 2010: 99), "Seeking to extend his mind toward the end of all ends, Augustine ultimately directs his gaze to the resurrected bodies unveiled in the heavenly city. Breathtakingly beautiful, infinitely desirable, these are bodies to die for, for they are bodies that will not die." He envisions all bodies, at whatever age and in whatever state they perished, to attain the same age, the prime of life, which Christ attained, in the resurrected life (*City of God*, 22.14–16). As for gender, Augustine contradicts Jerome's initial idea that women "will rise again as men": he asserts that in the resurrection life women will be "free of the necessity of intercourse and childbirth," essentially reversing the punishment of Eve, and that their "female organs" will be "part of a new beauty, which will not excite the lust of the beholder" (22.17). While the resurrected body will be free from deformity, irregularity, and ugliness, "harmonious" and hence beautiful in all of its parts, the wounds of the martyrs will still be visible, although any of their missing parts will be restored. Their scars will not be seen as "defects," but as "proof of their value" (22.19), just as Paul's sign of authentic apostleship was the "marks of Christ" branded on his body as Christ's slave (Gal 6:17). Nevertheless, Augustine differs from Paul in envisioning the nature of this restored body: it will be spiritual, but it will still be flesh, albeit a "spiritual flesh," created as it was intended to be prior to the Fall. The roles of flesh and spirit will not be reversed – they will be transformed: the flesh will no longer rule the "carnal spirit"; the spirit will rule the "spiritual flesh." The goal of the ascetic life on earth is thus achieved in the resurrection life, lived in the Heavenly City, where no one will be any longer enslaved to passion, and the desires of the flesh will at last be conquered (22.21, 30).

Abbreviations

Bibliography

Works Cited

Ancient Sources

Amat, Jacqueline (1996). *Passion de Perpétue et de Félicité suivi les Actes*. Sources Chrétiennes 417. Paris: Les Éditions du Cerf.

Ambrose. *Letters*. ET: http://newadvent.org/fathers/3409.htm

Ambrose. *On Virgins*. PL: 16: 197–243. ET: NPNF2: 10: 361–87.

Apocalypse of Peter (Coptic). Trans. James Brashler and Roger A. Bullard. (1976) *The Nag Hammadi Library in English*. Ed. James M. Robinson. San Francisco: HarperCollins. 373–8.

Augustine. *Concerning the City of God against the Pagans*. A New Translation by Henry Bettenson. (1984) Introduction by John O'Meara. London: Penguin Books.

Augustine. *On Marriage and Concupiscence*. PL 44.415–475. ET: NPNF1.5: 263–4.

Augustine, *Sermons*. PL 38 and 39. ET: *The Fathers of the Church: A New Translation*. Trans. Sister Mary S. Muldowney. (2015) Sagwan Press.

Basil of Ancyra. *On the True Integrity of Virginity*. PG 30.669–809.

Basil of Ancyra. A. Vaillant, ed. and trans. (1943) *De Virginitate de Saint Basile: Text view-Slave et traduction française*. Paris: Institut d'Études Slaves.

Brock, Sebastian, and Susan Ashbrook Harvey. (1987) *Holy Women of the Syrian Orient*. Berkeley: University of California Press.

Cicero. *On Invention, The Best Kind of Orator, Topics*. Book 2. Translated by H. M. Hubbell (1949). LCL, 386. Cambridge, MA: Harvard University Press.

Coptic Orthodox Church Network. *Commemorations for Toba 21:2: Departure of St. Hilaria, Daughter of Emperor Zeno*. www.copticchurch.net/synaxius/5_21/html

Cyprian. *On the Dress of Virgins*. PL4: 451–78.ET, ANF 5: 579–87.

Elliott, J. K. (1993) *The New Testament Apocrypha: A Collection of Apocryphal Christian Literature based on M.R. James*. Oxford: Clarendon Press.

Epiphanius. *Panarion (Medicine Box against Heresies)*. 2 vols. Trans. Frank Williams (1997, 1994). Leiden: Brill.

Euripides. *The Medea*. Translated by Rex Warner (1967). *The Complete Greek Tragedies*. Eds. David Grene and Richmond Lattimore: *Euripides I*. New York: Washington Square Press.

Eusebius. *History of the Christian Church (Historia ecclesiastica)*. ET: *NPNF*2. 1: 1–387.

Gregory of Nyssa. *Life of Macrina* PG 46: 462–998. ET: Trans. W. K. Lowther Clarke. (1916). London: SPCK.

Hennecke, Edgar, and Wilhelm Schneemelcher, eds. and trans. (1964–5). *New Testament Apocrypha*. 2 vols. Louisville, KY: Westminster Press.

Ignatius of Antioch. *To the Romans*. PG 5: 685–96.ET ANF 1: 73–78.

Jerome. *Against Jovinian*. PL 23: 221–352.ET: NPNF2. 6: 340–416.

Jerome. *Apology Against Rufinus*. PL 23: 415–514. ET: NPNF2. 3: 483–518.

Jerome. *Letters*. PL 30: 13–301.ET: NPNF2 3: 359–84.

John Chrysostom. *Homiles on Matthew*. http://newadvent.org/fathers/2001.htm

Justin Martyr. *First Apology, Second Apology*. ET: ANF 1: 136–270.

Marcus Aurelius (2006). *Meditations*. London: Penguin Classics.

Methodius. *Symposium (Banquet of the Ten Virgins)*. PG 18: 27–246.ET: ANF 6: 309–55.

Musurillo, Herbert, ed. and trans. (1972). *Acts of the Christian Martyrs*. Oxford: Clarendon Press.

Palladius. *Lausiac History*. PG 34: 995–1262.ET: Trans. W. K. Lowther Clarke (1918). London: SPCK.

Patterson, Stephen J., James M. Robinson, and Hans-Gebhard Gethge, eds. and trans. (1998). *The Fifth Gospel: The Gospel of Thomas Comes of Age*. Harrisburg, PA: Trinity Press International.

Plato. *Euthyphro, Apology, Crito, Phaedo, Phaedrus*. Trans. Harold North Fowler (1914). LCL, 36. Cambridge, MA: Harvard University Press,

Pliny the Younger. *Letters*. Volume I: Books 1–7. Trans. Betty Radice. (1969) LCL, 55. Cambridge, MA: Harvard University Press.

Pseudo-Athanasius. *The Life and Activity of the Holy and Blessed Teacher Syncletica*. Trans. Elizabeth Castelli (1990). In Vincent Wimbush, ed. *Ascetic Behavior in Greco-Roman Antiquity*. Minneapolis: Fortress Press.

Soranus. *Gynecology*. Trans. Owsei Tempkin (1956). Baltimore: Johns Hopkins University Press.

Suetonius. *Lives of the Caesars*, Volume II. Trans. J. C. Rolfe (1914). LCL, 39. Cambridge, MA: Harvard University Press.

Swan, Laura. (2001). *The Forgotten Desert Mothers: Sayings, Lives, and Stories of Early Christian Women*. New York: Paulist Press.

Tacitus. *Annals* 13–16. Trans. John Jackson (1937). LCL, 322. Cambridge, MA: Harvard University Press.

Tertullian. *Apologetic*. PL 3: 913–20.ET: ANF 4: 50–8.

Tertullian. *On Baptism*. PL 1: 305–34.ET: ANF 3: 181–235.

Tertullian. *On the Veiling of Virgins*. PL 2: 887–914.ET: ANF 4: 27–37.

Ward, Benedicta. (1987) *Harlots of the Desert: A Study of Repentance in Early Monastic Sources*. Oxford: A. R. Mowbray.

Modern Sources

Boyarin, Daniel. (1999). *Dying for God: Martyrdom and the Making of Christianity and Judaism*. Palo Alto: Stanford University Press.

Brown, Peter. (1982). *Society and the Holy in Late Antiquity*. Berkeley: University of California Press.

Bibliography   63

Brown, Peter. (1988). *The Body and Society: Men, Women, and Sexual Renunication in Early Christianity*. New York: Columbia University Press.

Buck, P. Lorraine. (2002). The Pagan Husband in Justin, '2 Apology' 2: 1–20. *JTS*, New series, 53 (2): 541–46.

Burkert, Walter. (1985). *Greek Religion*. Translated by John Raffan. Oxford: Basil Blackwell.

Burrus, Virginia. (1987). *Chastity as Autonomy: Women in the Stories of the Apocryphal Acts*. Lewiston/Queenston: Edwin Mellen Press.

Burrus, Virginia, Mark D. Jordan, and Karmen MacKendrick. (2010). *Seducing Augustine*. New York: Fordham University Press.

Castelli, Elizabeth. (2000). *Martyrdom and Memory: Early Christian Culture Making*. New York: Columbia University Press.

Castelli, Elizabeth. (1986). Virginity and Its Meaning for Women's Sexuality in Early Christianity. *JFSR* 2(1): 61–88.

Clark, Elizabeth. (1986). *Ascetic Piety and Women's Faith: Essays in Late Ancient Christianity*. Lewiston/Queenston: Edwin Mellen Press.

Clark, Elizabeth. (2008). The Celibate Bridegroom and His Virginal Brides: Metaphor and the Marriage of Jesus in Early Christian Ascetic Exegesis. *CH* 77 (19): 1–25.

Clark, Elizabeth. (1999). Melania the Elder. In *Augustine through the Ages: An Encyclopedia*. Ed. Allan D. Fitzgerald. Grand Rapids: Eerdmans, 1999, pp. 552–3.

Clark, Elizabeth. (1983). *Women in the Early Church: Message of the Fathers of the Church*. Wilmington, DE: Michael Glazier.

Cloke, Gillian. (1995). *This Female Man of God: Women and Spiritual Power in the Patristic Age, A.D. 350–450*. London: Routledge.

Cobb, L. Stephanie. (2016). *Divine Deliverance: Pain and Painlessness in Early Christian Martyr Texts*. Berkeley: University of California Press.

Cobb, L. Stephanie. (2008). *Dying to Be Men: Gender and Language in Early Christian Martyr Texts*. New York: Columbia University Press.

Cooper, Kate. (1996). *The Virgin and the Bride: Idealized Womanhood in Late Antiquity*. Cambridge, MA: Harvard University Press.

Dagron, Gilles. (1978). *Vie et miracles de sainte Thècle*. Brussels: Societé des Bollandistes.

Davies, Stevan L. (1980). *The Revolt of the Widows: The Social World of the Apocryphal Acts*. Carbondale: Southern Illinois University Press.

Davis, Stephen J. (2000). Crossed Texts, Crossed Sex: Intertextuality and Gender in Early Christian Legends of Holy Women Disguised as Men. *JECS* 10(1): 1–36.

Douglas, Mary. (1996). *Natural Symbols: Explorations in Cosmology*. 2nd ed. New York: Routledge.

Droge, Arthur J., and James D. Tabor. (1992). *A Noble Death: Suicide and Martyrdom among Christians and Jews in Antiquity*. San Francisco: HarperCollins.

Elliott, Alison Goddard. (1988). *Roads to Paradise: Reading the Lives of the Early Saints*. Hanover, NH: University Press of New England for Brown University Press.

Glancy, Jennifer. (2002). *Slavery in Early Christianity*. Oxford: Oxford University Press.

Hunink, Vincent. (2016). Did Perpetua Write Her Passion Account? *Listy filologiké/Folia philologica*, 133 (1/2): 147–55.

Hylen, Susan. (2015). *A Modest Apostle: Thecla and the History of Women in the Early Church*. Oxford: Oxford University Press.

Kateusz, Ally. (2013). Collyridian Déjà Vu: The Trajectory of Redaction of the Markers of Mary's Liturgical Leadership. *JFSR* 29 (2): 75–92.

Kateusz, Ally. (2019). *Mary and Early Christian Women: Hidden Leadership*. London: Palgrave MacMillan.

Kitts, Margo. (2018). The *Martys* and Spectacular Death: From Homer to the Roman Arena. *Journal of Religion and Violence*, 6 (2): 267–84.

Kraemer, Ross S. (2011). *Unreliable Witnesses: Religion, Gender, and History in the Greco-Roman Mediterranean*. Oxford: Oxford University Press.

Kyle, Donald. (1998). *Spectacles of Death in Ancient Rome*. London: Routledge.

Loraux, Nicole. (1985). *Tragic Ways of Killing a Woman*. Trans. Anthony Forster. Cambridge, MA: Harvard University Press.

MacDonald, Dennis R. (1985). *The Legend and the Apostle: The Battle for Paul in Story and Canon*. Philadelphia: Westminster Press.

McLarty, J. D. (2018) *Thecla's Devotion: Narrative, Emotion, and Identity in the* Acts of Paul and Thecla. Cambridge: James Clarke.

Miles, Margaret R. (2013). *Recollections and Reconsiderations*. San Francisco: Harper One.

Moss, Candida R. (2019). *Divine Bodies: Resurrecting Perfection in the New Testament and Early Christianity*. New Haven: Yale University Press.

Moss, Candida R. (2013). *The Myth of Persecution: How Early Christians Invented a Story of Martyrdom*. San Francisco: Harper One.

Moss, Candida R. (2010). *The Other Christs: Imitating Jesus in Ancient Christian Ideologist of Martyrdom*. Oxford: Oxford University Press.

Murphy, Francis X. (1947). Melania the Elder: A Biographical Note. *Traditio*, 3: 59–77.

Rosario Rodriguez, Rubén. (2017). *Christian Martyrdom and Political Violence: A Comparative Theology with Judaism and Islam*. Cambridge: Cambridge University Press.

Rousselle, Aline. (1988). *Porneia: On Desire and the Body in Antiquity*. Trans. Felicia Pheasant. Oxford: Basil Blackwell.

Salisbury, Joyce E. (1991). *Church Fathers: Independent Virgins*. London: Verso.

Scarry, Elaine. (1985). *The Body in Pain: The Making and Unmaking of the World*. New York: Oxford University Press.

Schüssler Fiorenza, Elisabeth. (1983.) *In Memory of Her: A Feminist Reconstruction of Christian Origins*. New York: Crossroads.

Shaw, Brent D. (1996). Body/Power/Identity: Passions of the Martyrs. *JECS* 4 (3): 269–312.

Shaw, Teresa. (1998). *The Burden of the Flesh: Fasting and Sexuality in Early Christianity*. Minneapolis: Fortress Press.

Streete, Gail. (1998). *Askesis* and Resistance in the Pastoral Letters. In Leif Vaage and Vincent Wimbush, eds., *Asceticism in the New Testament*. New York: Routledge, 299–316.

Streete, Gail. (2005). Authority and Authorship: *The Acts of Paul and Thecla* as a Disputed Pauline Text. *LTQ*, 40 (4): 265–76.

Streete, Gail. (2006). Buying the Stairway to Heaven: Perpetua and Thecla as Early Christian Heroines. In A.-J. Levine, ed., with Maria Mayo Robbins, *A Feminist Companion to the New Testament Apocrypha*. London: T & T Clark International, 186–215.

Streete, Gail. (1986). The Divine Woman? Propaganda and the Power of Chastity in the New Testament Apocrypha. In *Rescuing Creusa*, Marilyn B. Skinner, ed. *Helios* 13 (2): 151–62.

Streete, Gail. (2018). Performing Christian Martyrdoms. In Margo Kitts, ed. *Martyrdom, Self-Sacrifice, and Self-Immolation*. Oxford: Oxford University Press, 40–53.

Streete, Gail. (2009). *Redeemed Bodies: Women Martyrs in Early Christianity*. Louisville, KY: Westminster John Knox Press.

Streete, Gail. (1999). Women as Sources of Redemption and Knowledge in Early Christian Tradition. In Ross S. Kraemer and Mary Rose D'Angelo, eds. *Women and Christian Origins*. New York: Oxford University Press, 330–54.

Vander Stichele, Caroline and Todd Penner. (2009). *Contextualizing Gender in Early Christian Discourse: Thinking Beyond Thecla*. London: T & T Clark.

Wilson-Kastner, Patricia, et al. (1981). *A Lost Tradition: Women Writers of the Early Church*. Lanham, MD: University Press of America.

For Further Reading

The Apocryphal Acts of the Apostles. Guest ed., Dennis R. MacDonald. (1986). *Semeia* 38. Atlanta: Scholars Press.

The Apostolic Fathers. (2004). Ed. Bart D. Ehrman. Vols. 1 & 2. LCL 24 & 25. Cambridge: Harvard University Press.

Asceticism. Vincent L. Wimbush and Richard R. Valantasis, eds., with the assistance of Gay Byron and William S. Love. (1995). Oxford: Oxford University Press.

Boughton, Lynne C. (1991). From Pious Legend to Feminist Fantasy. *JR* 71 (3): 362–83.

Bremmer, Jan, ed. (1996). *The Apocryphal Acts of Paul and Thecla*. Louvain: Peeters.

Bremmer, Jan, and Marco Formisano. (2012). *Perpetua's Passions: Multidisciplinary Approaches to the Passio Perpetuae et Felicitatis*. Oxford: Oxford University Press.

Cardman, Francis. (1988). Acts of the Women Martyrs. *AThR*, 70 (2): 144–50.

Changing Bodies, Changing Meanings: Studies on the Human Body in Antiquity. Ed. Dominic Montserrat. New York: Columbia University Press.

Clark, Elizabeth A. (1998). Holy Women, Holy Words: Early Christian Women, Social History, and the "Linguistic Turn." *JECS*, 6 (3): 413–30.

Clark, Elizabeth A. (1994). Ideology, History, and the Construction of "Woman" in Late Antique Christianity. JECS, 2 (2): 155–84.

D'Angelo, Mary Rose. (2003). *Eusebeia*: Roman Imperial Family Values and the Sexual Politics of 4 Maccabees and the Pastorals. *BibInt*, 11 (2): 139–265.

Davis, Sephen J. (2001). *The Cult of Saint Thecla: A Tradition of Women's Piety in Late Antiquity*. Oxford: Oxford University Press.

Elm, Susannah. (1994). *"Virgins of God": The Making of Asceticism in Late Antiquity*. Oxford: Clarendon Press.

Harvey, Susan Ashbrook. (2008). Martyr Passions and Hagiography. In *The Oxford Handbook of Early Christian Studies*. Ed. Susan A. Harvey and David Hunter. Oxford: Oxford University Press, 603–27.

Heffernan, Thomas J. (2012). *The Passion of Perpetual and Felicity*. Oxford: Oxford University Press.

Johnson, Scott Fitzgerald. (2006). *The Life and Miracles of Saint Thekla: A Literary Study*. Hellenic Studies 13. Washington, DC: Center for Hellenic Studies.

Kraemer, Ross Shepard. (1980). The Conversion of Women to Ascetic Forms of Christianity. *Signs* 6: 298–307.

Kraemer, Ross Shepard, ed. (1988). *Maenads, Martyrs, Matrons, and Monastics: A Sourcebook on Women's Religions in the Ancient World*. Philadelphia: Fortress.

Kraemer, Ross Shepard, and Mary Rose D'Angelo, eds. (1999). *Women and Christian Origins*. New York: Oxford University Press.

Lefkowitz, Mary R. (1976). The Motivations for St. Perpetua's Martyrdom. *JAAR*, 44 (3): 417–21.

Levine, Amy-Jill, ed.,with Maria Mayo Robbins. (2006). *A Feminist Companion to the New Testament Apocrypha*. London: T&T Clark.

MacDonald, Margaret Y. (1996). *Early Christian Women and Pagan Opinion: The Power of the Hysterical Woman*. Cambridge: Cambridge University Press.

Matthews, Shelly. (2001). Thinking of Thecla: Issues in Feminist Historiography. *JFSR*, 17 (2): 39–55.

Miles, Margaret R. (1989). *Carnal Knowing: Female Nakedness and Religious Meaning in the Christian West*. Boston: Beacon.

Miller, Patricia Cox. (2005). *Women in Early Christianity: Translations from Greek Texts*. Washington, DC: Catholic University of America Press.

Perkins, Judith B. (1995). *The Suffering Self: Pain and Narrative Representation in the Early Christian Era*. London: Routledge.

Ronsse, Erin. (2006). Rhetoric of Martyrs: Listening to Saints Perpetua and Felicitas. *JECS*, 14 (3): 283–97.

Salisbury, Joyce E. (1997). *Perpetua's Passion: The Death and Memory of a Young Roman Woman*. New York: Routledge.

Scarry, Elaine. (1985). *The Body in Pain: The Making and Unmaking of the World*. New York: Oxford University Press.

Schüssler Fiorenza, Elisabeth, ed. (1994). *Searching the Scriptures*, vol. 2, *A Feminist Commentary*. New York: Crossroad.

Shaw, Brent D. (1993). The Passion of Perpetua – Christian Women Martyred in Carthage in A.D. 203. *Past and Present* 56: 3–45.

Tilley, Maureen A. (1991). The Ascetic Body and the (Un)Making of the World of the Martyr. *JAAR*, 59 (3): 467–79.

Van Henten, Jan Willem, and Friedrich Avemarie. (2002). *Martyrdom and Noble Death: Selected Texts from Graeco-Roman, Jewish, and Christian Antiquity*. London: Routledge.

Young, Robin Darling. (1991). The Woman with the Soul of Abraham: Traditions about the Mother of the Maccabaean Martyrs. In *"Women Like This": New Perspectives on Jewish Women in the Greco-Roman World*. Ed. Amy-Jill Levine. Atlanta: Scholars Press, 67–81.

Cambridge Elements ⹀

Religion and Violence

James R. Lewis
Wuhan University

James R. Lewis is Professor at Wuhan University, and the author and editor of a number of volumes, including *The Cambridge Companion to Religion and Terrorism*.

Margo Kitts
Hawai'i Pacific University

Margo Kitts edits the *Journal of Religion and Violence* and is Professor and Coordinator of Religious Studies and East-West Classical Studies at Hawai'i Pacific University in Honolulu.

About the Series
Violence motivated by religious beliefs has become all too common in the years since the 9/11 attacks. Not surprisingly, interest in the topic of religion and violence has grown substantially since then. This Elements series on Religion and Violence addresses this new, frontier topic in a series of ca. fifty individual Elements. Collectively, the volumes will examine a range of topics, including violence in major world religious traditions, theories of religion and violence, holy war, witch hunting, and human sacrifice, among others.

Cambridge Elements ≡

Religion and Violence

Made in the USA
Middletown, DE
11 November 2023

42402078R00046